MW01264548

"Fascinating. With candor and compassion, Christopher Yuan combines personal history, impressive research, biblical insights and practical recommendations to sexuality on the campuses of Christian colleges and universities. This is the book to read on Christian faith and sexual identity at Christian colleges. *Giving a Voice to the Voiceless* is a book for every campus constituency from students to presidents, administrators, alumni, faculty, parents, trustees, donors and more!"

—LEITH ANDERSON
President, National Association of Evangelicals

"Christopher Yuan has done careful research on the experience of students who navigate their same sex attraction or orientation at Christian colleges and universities. His wise and practical recommendations—firmly rooted in a faithful biblical ethic for human sexuality—will help campus leaders care for all of their students with truth and grace."

—PHILIP RYKEN
President, Wheaton College

"*Giving a Voice to the Voiceless* is an invaluable study of the experiences of college students who struggle with same-sex attraction on well-meaning Christian college campuses. Indeed the glossary alone is worth the price of the book. Faithful, biblical students who hold to a traditional view of sexuality and who struggle with SSA are even more voiceless today than they were years ago, as the rise of LGBT rights on college campuses does not speak for faithful Christians or reflect the complex emotions and challenges that students face. This book is a healing balm for these students and will edify, equip, and encourage. It is a must-read book for every college administrator."

—ROSARIA BUTTERFIELD
Author; Speaker

"Based on a pioneering study, this book provides relevant insights and counsel for Christian colleges and universities seeking to walk compassionately and faithfully with LGB and SSA students. As one who knows both the Christian and gay communities, Christopher Yuan has listened well and now is uniquely able to speak to both of them with grace and truth. For anyone who wants to understand better the experiences of students grappling with issues of sexual identity at Christian institutions, this book should be required reading."

—D. MICHAEL LINDSAY
President, Gordon College

"Once more Christopher Yuan has come along side those of us who are seeking guidance in navigating the increasingly complex waters of human sexuality. Solidly biblical, relentlessly compassionate and appropriately practical, this book will be noted far and wide for its important contribution to individuals, churches, and Christian colleges and universities who want to honor Christ by embracing the marginalized in His name."

—JOSEPH M. STOWELL III
President, Cornerstone University

"There will be no bigger challenge to leaders of Christian colleges and universities in the next decade than the skillful navigation of issues surrounding human sexuality. Christopher Yuan provides careful research to help guide leaders through the many landmines with both biblical integrity and godly compassion. I strongly urge college presidents, administrators and trustees to read, digest, and incorporate this important material."

—J. PAUL NYQUIST
President, Moody Bible Institute

"Those of us who have served as leaders in Christ-centered universities know the tsunami effect of cultural changes that force us to respond. None are more divisive than the core issues of homosexuality. With a growing number of LGB students attending even the most conservative colleges, Christopher Yuan has provided a way forward for us. His biblical understanding, qualitative research, and 34 action steps provide a substantive and practical plan for the entire campus."

—WILLIAM E. BROWN
Former President, Cedarville University; Current Senior Fellow
of Worldview and Culture, The Colson Center for Christian Worldview

"Christopher is an aspirational model for us all. He is deeply grounded in the truth of the gospel while also willing to embrace the journey of complete surrender to the call of Jesus and his model of grace to all, most especially our marginalized neighbors whom we are called to love as ourselves. Christopher's research, findings, and action steps are both a call and an invaluable resource to the voice of the voiceless in the faith community."

—DAVID A. KING
President, Malone University

"With his book, *Giving a Voice to the Voiceless*, Christopher Yuan has made a significant contribution to the discussions surrounding LGB and same-sex attracted students at Christian colleges and universities. He offers a compassionate account of and thoughtful advice on how Christian colleges can respond to the experiences of students navigating important questions related to their sexual identity."

—**MARK A. YARHOUSE**
Hughes Endowed Chair & Professor of Psychology of Regent University

"Christopher Yuan's research and recommendations come at an important time for those of us who serve in Christian higher education. What we have heard anecdotally and directly from LGBT students is confirmed by his research; but more importantly his insights and recommendations provide tangible "next steps" so all students can thrive and live well in our campus communities. Thanks Christopher for your thoughtful help with our students who face challenging realities related to their sexuality."

—**EDEE SCHULZE**
Vice President for Student Life, Dean of Students, Westmont College;
President Elect of the Association for Christians in Student Development

"No amount of denial can obscure the fact that both same-sex attracted (SSA) and self-identifying or practicing LGB students are enrolled in even North America's most conservative Christian colleges. Christopher Yuan's exceedingly candid and timely research thoughtfully illuminates why and how our Christian college communities should care for these marginalized students."

—**RALPH E. ENLOW, JR.**
President of Association for Biblical Higher Education

"Christopher Yuan has taken his real life journey, viewed it from a biblical and God-focused worldview, and created a functional path for today's Christian institutions to begin to lovingly minister and walk with the LGBTQ individuals that populate their campuses. This is a call to Christian higher education, but also the church of Christ, to break down walls without compromising the gospel and teachings of Christ."

—**DAN WOOD**
Executive Director of National Christian College Athletic Association

Giving a Voice to the
Voiceless

Giving a Voice to the
—— Voiceless ——

A Qualitative Study of Reducing
Marginalization of Lesbian, Gay, Bisexual,
and Same-Sex Attracted Students at Christian
Colleges and Universities

Christopher Yuan

WIPF & STOCK · Eugene, Oregon

GIVING A VOICE TO THE VOICELESS
A Qualitative Study of Reducing Marginalization of Lesbian, Gay, Bisexual, and Same-sex Attracted Students at Christian Colleges and Universities

Wipf & Stock
An Imprint of Wipf and Stock Publishers
199 W. 8th Ave., Suite 3
Eugene, OR 97401

www.wipfandstock.com

PAPERBACK ISBN: 978-1-4982-8925-2
HARDCOVER ISBN: 978-1-4982-8927-6

Manufactured in the U.S.A.

To Dad and Mom
Your sacrifices and servant hearts made this all possible

Contents

Figures

Tables

Acknowledgments

M ORE THAN ANYTHING ELSE, I praise God for placing me on this journey of sweet surrender to the Lord Jesus, which started sixteen years ago. I must thank those who helped me finish my doctoral thesis, from which this book was based. I deeply appreciate the wise direction of my thesis advisor, Katie Friesen Smith, who guided me through the doctoral research process. Thanks to my second reader, Edee Schulze, whose bimonthly phone calls kept me moving forward. You selflessly shared your wisdom and experience from the student development world as I shaped this research. Steve Ivester assisted me with figuring out the data analysis software. I also cannot forget those at Bethel Seminary who aided me in the doctorate of ministry program: Justin Irving, Sam Rima, Tim Senapatiratne, Steve Sandage, John Sanders, Ceallaigh Anderson, and Renae Long. My thesis editor, Darlene Colwell, was fantastic and had a keen eye for the technical details.

In addition, I am grateful for all who sacrificially and promptly assisted to transform my DMin thesis into a book. Thanks to Joseph Torres, Nathan Sundt, Julie Gurgone, Jennifer Hutmire, Neal Anderson, Steve Ivester, Brad Lau, Bill Brown, Deb Crater, and Lawrence Kimbrough for helping me on such short notice. I give a special thanks to Judy Hagey and Linda Au Parker for tirelessly tagging and proofreading the entire manuscript. I am grateful to Wipf and Stock Publishers for their courage and foresight to publish this much needed resource.

I am very grateful to my two closest friends. Joe Hendrickson, thanks for your courageous honesty and fearless intimacy through all these years. Rosaria Butterfield, you are an older sister that I never had. Your weekly phone calls sharpen me and praying together with you enriches my spirit.

Acknowledgments

Lastly, I am truly indebted to my parents, Leon and Angela Yuan. They spoiled me by taking care of many details (cooking, laundry, etc.) in order that I could focus on writing. Without their persistent exhortations to stay on track, I would never have finished. Words cannot express how thankful I am that I have such wonderful parents as you. This book is dedicated to you both.

Abbreviations

BDAG	Bauer, Danker, Arndt, and Gingrich, *Greek-English Lexicon of the New Testament*
BDB	Brown, Driver, and Briggs, *Hebrew and English Lexicon*
ESV	English Standard Version
GLAAD	Gay and Lesbian Alliance Against Defamation
GSA	Gay Straight Alliance
HALOT	*The Hebrew and Aramaic Lexicon of the Old Testament*
IRB	Institutional Review Board
LGB	Lesbian, gay, bisexual
LGBT	Lesbian, gay, bisexual, transgender
LSJ	Liddell, Scott, and Jones, *A Greek-English Lexicon*
LXX	Septuagint (Greek translation of the Hebrew Old Testament)
NASB	New American Standard Bible
NIDNTTE	*New International Dictionary of New Testament Theology and Exegesis*
NIDOTTE	*New International Dictionary of Old Testament Theology and Exegesis*
NIV	New International Version
PVS	Progressive view of sexuality

Abbreviations

RA	Resident assistant (dormitory)
SSA	Same-sex attracted
TDNT	*Theological Dictionary of the New Testament*
TDOT	*Theological Dictionary of the Old Testament*
TVS	Traditional view of sexuality
TWOT	*Theological Wordbook of the Old Testament*

Glossary

Alienation—Refers to either objective conditions or subjective feelings that discourage participation or inclusion, and distance or estrange an individual or a group from another individual or group.[1] Also refers to the distancing of people from experiencing a crystallized totality both in the social world and in the self.[2] The opposite of alienation is recognition.

Asexual—A person who lacks desire for or has a low interest in sex.

Bisexual—An individual who is sexually and/or romantically attracted to men and women. The author believes this term should be used to describe one's attractions and/or actions, and not to describe one's identity.

Campus climate—The atmosphere or environment of a college or university, both in and out of the classroom, that fosters or impedes full academic, personal, and professional development of underprivileged or underrepresented people groups within an academic community.[3] The current attitudes, behaviors, and standards of faculty, staff, administrators, and students concerning the level of respect for individual needs, abilities, and potential.[4]

---

1. Kalekin-Fishman, "Tracing the Growth of Alienation," 97.
2. Kalekin-Fishman, *Designs for Alienation*, 6.
3. Hall and Sandler, *The Campus Climate*, 2.
4. Regents of the University of California, "What is campus climate?"

Glossary

Celibate—Remaining sexually abstinent for life or for an extended period of time. A person often intentionally makes a vow or is called by God to live in this manner. Some view celibacy to be a vocation.[5]

Christian colleges and universities—Private institutions of higher education that are distinctively Christian in nature. Although not all of these institutions require their students to be Christian, most require students to agree to a lifestyle agreement, which reserve sexual intimacy to be between a husband and a wife.

Closeted—Describes a person who is not open about her or his sexual orientation.

Coming out—Refers to several aspects of the experiences of lesbian, gay, bisexual, and same-sex attracted people, such as: self-awareness of same-sex attractions; the telling of one or a few people about these attractions; widespread disclosure of same-sex attractions; and identification with the lesbian, gay, and bisexual community.[6]

Gay—Describes a person with enduring physical, romantic, and/or emotional attractions to people of the same sex.[7] The author believes this term should be used to describe one's attractions and/or actions, and not to describe one's identity.

Heteronormative—A term used by advocates of LGB rights referring to the practices and policies that are believed to reinforce heterosexuality, heterosexual relationships, the male/female binary, and traditional gender roles. In addition, it is believed that heteronormativity reinforces heterosexuality as the normative and natural sexuality[8] and anything other than opposite-sex intimate relationships as not normative. This is mostly used as a pejorative term by those who affirm gay relationships or identify as LGB.

Heterosexism—A term used by advocates of LGB rights referring to an ideology found in institutional practices or individual relationships that works to the disadvantage of lesbian, gay, and bisexual people.[9]

5. Belgau, "Vocation Roundup."

6. American Psychological Association, *Answers to Your Questions*.

7. Gay and Lesbian Alliance Against Defamation, *Media Reference Guide*, 6.

8. Lovaas and Jenkins, *Sexualities and Communication*, 98; Berlant and Warner, "Sex in Public," 312.

9. Herek et al., "Internalized Stigma among Sexual Minority Adults," 33; Stratton et al., "Sexual Minorities in Faith-Based Higher Education," 4.

Like heteronormativity, this is mostly used as a pejorative term by those who affirm gay relationships or identify as LGB. It is an alternative to homophobia equating heterosexism to sexism and racism.[10] Advocates believe that heterosexism enforces strict adherence to gender role stereotypes and maintains gender oppression.[11]

Heterosexual—Describes a person who is attracted to people of the opposite sex. The author believes this term should be used to describe one's attractions and/or actions, and not to describe one's identity.

Homophobia—Antipathy and prejudice toward gay, lesbian, or bisexual people and/or homosexuality in general.

Homosexual—Although this word has commonly been used to refer to gay and lesbian people, it is considered to be a more clinical and impersonal term. Therefore for some, this term is offensive and they prefer gay or lesbian. The author believes this term should be used to describe one's attractions and/or actions, and not to describe one's identity.

Homosexual behavior—Refers to sexual intimacy between two people of the same sex. Sexual intimacy is any activity that can lead to orgasm, including but not limited to vaginal sex, anal sex, oral sex, "dry" sex, mutual masturbation, fondling, or deep kissing. For many gay, lesbian, and bisexual people, homosexual behavior is an offensive term because, to them, their sexuality is not a behavior but their identity. In addition, some believe the term "behavior" is vague and imprecise.

Institutional oppression—A term used by activists referring to the systematic oppression and/or mistreatment of individuals of a particular social identity group. This is supported and enforced by society and institutions based only upon the individual's membership in a particular social identity group.[12]

LGB—Acronym for "lesbian, gay, and bisexual." Also GLB. The more inclusive and current acronym is LGBTQIA (lesbian, gay, bisexual, transgender, queer, questioning, intersex, asexual, and ally).

10. McGeorge and Carlson, "Deconstructing Heterosexism," 14.

11. Kitzinger, "Sexualities," 277.

12. Cheney et al., "Institutionalized Oppression Definitions."

Lesbian—Describes a woman with enduring physical, romantic, and/or emotional attractions to other women.[13] The author believes this term should be used to describe one's attractions and/or actions, and not to describe one's identity.

Lifestyle—A term often used by conservative Christians to describe how LGB people live. However, it is often offensive to LGB people and should be avoided. Just as there is not a straight lifestyle representing all straight people, there is not a gay lifestyle representing all gay people.

Lifestyle agreement—Some Christian colleges require all students to sign an agreement that articulates how students are expected to live and behave. Influenced by a traditional Christian ethic, these policies often include policies regarding sexual purity, such as no sexual relations outside the context of a husband and wife in marriage (adultery, fornication, homosexual behavior, etc.). Also called Community Covenant or Student Life Guide.

Marginalization—A multidimensional process of progressive social rupture, detaching groups and individuals from social relations and institutions and preventing them from full participation in the normal, normatively prescribed activities of the society in which they live. This is also known as social exclusion.[14] To marginalize is to relegate to an unimportant or powerless position within a society or group.[15]

Non-heterosexual—People who do not identify as heterosexual, such as LGB. For some, this term moves beyond the binary definitions of "straight" and LGB.[16] Dilley further clarifies that non-heterosexual is defined as "sexual and/or affectional relationships with members of the same gender."[17] Some consider this term unsatisfactory because it reinforces heterosexuality as the norm (see heteronormativity).[18] But for the sake of this research, non-heterosexual was initially chosen for the questionnaire as a more inclusive way of referring both to those who identify as gay, lesbian, or bisexual, as well as to those who expe-

13. GLAAD, *Media Reference Guide*, 7.
14. Silver, "Social Exclusion," 15.
15. Merriam-Webster Online Dictionary, "Marginalize."
16. Dilley, *Queer Man on Campus*, 4.
17. Dilley, 9.
18. Yip, "Queering Religious Texts," 32.

rience same-sex attractions and may not embrace a gay identity. Also for the sake of this research, non-heterosexual does not include gender dysphoria and transgenderism. This is not a commonly used term.

Openly gay—Describes a person who self-identifies as lesbian or gay in one's public and/or professional lives (also openly lesbian or openly bisexual). However, those who identify as LGB often do not like the term "openly gay" and prefer simply "gay."

Pansexual—A person who is sexually and/or romantically attracted toward people of any gender identity or biological sex. Pansexual people sometimes refer to themselves as being gender blind, in which gender and sex are insignificant or irrelevant to their sexual or romantic attractions.

Progressive view of sexuality—This perspective posits that homosexual acts are not in themselves immoral or sinful but, like heterosexual acts, are good or bad depending on the context that defines and gives meaning to them.[19] For the sake of this research, the acronym PVS will be used.

Queer—An identity without essence, not a condition but a horizon of possibilities, fluidity in gender and sexuality that can change to and from over time.[20]

Safe Space—A place usually in public/secular schools, colleges, or universities that is open and accepting of LGBT people and affirming of same-sex relationships. In these safe spaces, "anti-LGBT sentiment" is not tolerated and there is no fear of feeling uncomfortable, unwelcome, or unsafe on account of one's sexual or gender identity.[21]

Same-sex attracted (SSA)—A subjective experience of emotional, romantic, and/or sexual attractions to the same sex.[22] Those who identify as LGB do not normally use this term. Rather, it is a term used by those who believe that homosexual sex and romantic relationships should not be pursued and do not want to identify as LGB. How one may use this term would be, "I struggle with same-sex attractions" or "I have same-sex attractions." For some, this places less emphasis upon their

19. Via and Gagnon, *Homosexuality and the Bible*, 1.

20. Halperin, *Saint Foucault*, 79.

21. Advocates for Youth, "Glossary."

22. Yarhouse, "Sex Attraction, Homosexual Orientation, and Gay Identity," 202.

sexual attractions and more emphasis upon their faith. This term is of-fensive to some who do identify as LGB. For the sake of this research, the noun form, same-sex attraction, was not used and the adjectival form, same-sex attracted, was used.

Same-sex sexuality—Refers to all experiences of same-sex desire, roman-tic affections, fantasy, or behavior.[23] Same-sex sexuality can be used to describe those who do not identify as lesbian, gay, or bisexual but experience same-sex attractions, as well as those who do identify as lesbian, gay, or bisexual. Same-sex sexuality is independent from whether one experiences any opposite sex sexuality (desire, behavior, or identity).[24] This is not a commonly used term.

Sexual behavior—Refers to actual sexual acts performed by an individual.

Sexual identity— Refers to how one thinks of oneself in terms of whom one is sexually and romantically attracted to.[25] Sexual identity and sexual behavior are related, but different. Identity refers to an indi-vidual's concept of themselves. Behavior refers to actual sexual acts performed by the individual. Sexual identity appears to entail biologi-cal sex (male or female), gender identity (psychological sense of being male or female), sex role (social expectations for one's sex), sexual orientation and intention/valuative framework (how one intends to live in light of one's beliefs and values).[26]

Sexual minority—Refers to individuals who are not from the sexual majority (i.e., heterosexual people)[27] and who experience same-sex attractions or engage in same-sex sexual behavior, regardless of self-identification.[28] This term includes those who identify as gay, lesbian, or bisexual, as well as those who experience same-sex attractions and may not embrace a gay identity. The weakness of this term is that it draws a correlation between sexual minorities and racial minorities. Sexual minority can also denote transgender people and those who experience gender dysphoria. However, this research did not focus on transgenderism.

23. Diamond, *Sexual Fluidity*, 13.
24. Stratton et al., 17.
25. Feminism and Women's Studies, "Sexual Identity and Gender Identity Glossary."
26. Yarhouse et al., "Sexual Identity Development and Synthesis," 3.
27. Ullerstam, *The Erotic Minorities*.
28. Diamond, "A Dynamical Systems Approach," 142.

Sexual orientation—Refers to the direction, persistence, and/or enduring pattern of one's emotional, romantic, and/or sexual attractions to men, women, or both sexes.[29] This generally consists of at least three dimensions: identity, behaviors, and attractions.[30] The researcher prefers to define sexual orientation as the capacity or potentiality for a person to have physical, romantic, and/or emotional attractions toward the opposite and/or same sex. Sexual orientation is preferred over "sexual preference," which can be offensive to LGB people, suggesting that being gay or lesbian is voluntary and therefore "curable."[31]

Singleness—The state of being unmarried. A single person can be never married, divorced, widowed, or separated. For some, singleness is volitional, but often it is not. Although the Bible expects those who are single to abstain from sexual intimacy, not all singles remain sexually abstinent.

Snowball sampling—A sampling technique where existing research participants recruit future subjects from among their own acquaintances. This technique is often used to access hidden populations, which are difficult for researchers to access. The researcher must find an insider who is a member of the group studied and is willing to be an informant, acting as a guide.[32]

Straight—Describes a person who is attracted to people of the opposite sex.

Student Development, Department of—A department at a postsecondary educational campus that aids students in holistic change, growth, and development by providing programs, services, resources, and interventions. Often residence life (housing and dorms) is included in this area. This is sometimes called Student Affairs or Student Life.

Traditional view of sexuality—This perspective posits that the Bible condemns same-sex sexual practice and romantic relationships, and that God only blesses marriage between a husband and a wife. All

29. Yarhouse et al., "Sexual Identity," 3; APA, *Answers.*
30. Haas et al., "Suicide and Suicide Risk," 10–51.
31. GLAAD, *Media Reference Guide,* 7.
32. Denzin and Lincoln, *Collecting and Interpreting Qualitative Materials,* 77.

homosexual acts are sinful by their very nature.[33] For the sake of this research, the acronym TVS will be used.

33. Via and Gagnon, 1.

1

Research Problem and Design

THERE IS A GREAT need and even urgency to address the sense of marginalization of lesbian, gay, bisexual (LGB), and same-sex attracted (SSA) students at Christian colleges and universities. Current events necessitate this. In the fall of 2015, the president of the University of Missouri, Tim Wolfe, resigned amid controversy surrounding his perceived failure to address marginalization and institutional oppression of African-American students.[1] Student activism at this university received broad national media attention. A graduate student started a hunger strike, university faculty discussed the possibility of a walkout, and the campus football team threatened to go on strike. The events at the University of Missouri became a catalyst for student protests at campuses around the country with some even demanding resignations of other top administrators. There were protests at Princeton University, Occidental College, Georgetown University, Yale University, Claremont McKenna College, Ithaca College, Johns Hopkins University, University of Alabama, Purdue University, and Vanderbilt University.[2] The institutional oppression and marginalization addressed at these different protests focused not only on racism and feminism, but also heterosexism. Will Christian colleges and universities be next in the national spotlight due to a perceived lack of response to institutional oppression and marginalization of non-heterosexual students? Most institutions of Christian higher education realize the need to reduce the marginaliza-

1. Gallion and Coleman, "MSA Letter to Curators."
2. Pauly and Andrews, "Campus Protests Are Spreading."

1

tion of LGB and SSA students, but do not have a resource to help them with the answer. This research was accomplished to be a resource to help Christian colleges and universities find ways in which to reduce marginalization of LGB and SSA students while still holding fast to a traditional view of sexuality.

The impetus for this study began in 2006, when Soulforce visited sixteen Christian colleges and universities to protest their policies against same-sex sexual practice, which they believe these policies lead to the marginalization of LGB and SSA students.[3] Mel White, who had been a ghostwriter for Jerry Falwell, Billy Graham, Pat Robertson, and others, came out as a gay man and founded Soulforce, a civil rights and social justice group. The purpose was to "challenge the religious right through relentless nonviolent resistance in order to end the political and religious oppression of LGBTQI people."[4] Although uninvited, some schools did engage the activists, and the conversation on sexuality began and continued at these Christian colleges and universities. In addition, several LGB alumni formed alumni groups and expressed their painful experiences and sense of marginalization while at their respective Christian colleges or universities. Many felt marginalized as if they had no voice. These LGB alumni wanted their college to see the harm caused to them and prevent other LGB students from experiencing the same pain. Their conclusion was to eliminate the institutional policies against same-sex sexual practice.

Many non-Christians believe that an institutional policy against same-sex sexual practice is discriminatory. In 2012, Trinity Western University (TWU), a private Christian liberal arts university in British Columbia, Canada, submitted a proposal to offer a juris doctor program. However, three provinces (Nova Scotia, Ontario, and British Columbia) refused to automatically accredit potential graduates based solely upon TWU's institutional policy against same-sex sexual practice.[5] The university has taken all three provincial law societies to court. As of the beginning of 2016, all three cases were pending appeals and will most likely head to the Supreme Court of Canada for decision.[6] In 2014, the president of Gordon College was one of fourteen leaders from religious and civic organizations that signed a letter to President Obama requesting a religious exemption for

3. Pulliam, "Gay Rights Group Targets Christian Colleges."

4. Soulforce, "Our Story."

5. Robertson, "Trinity Western University Ready."

6. Mulgrew, "B.C. Supreme Court Rules."

his "planned executive order addressing federal contractors and LGBT employment policies."[7] Somehow, this letter was released to the public and reposted on national newspaper outlets. As a result, the mayor of Salem, Massachusetts, ended the city's contract with the college that had allowed the college to manage and maintain the Old Town Hall. The mayor explained that Gordon's institutional policies against same-sex sexual practice "fly in the face" of the city's non-discrimination ordinance.[8] In addition, Lynn Public Schools severed its ties with the college so that students were no longer allowed to fulfill their degree requirements in social work and education at these public schools.[9] Most of these objections stemmed from a misunderstanding of the institutional policies as discriminatory and harmful. Although prohibiting same-sex sexual behavior, these policies did not bar a student for simply *being* LGB or SSA. And yet, students at Christian colleges and universities do report a sense of marginalization while enrolled at their school.

The secular community, gay rights activists, and LGB alumni groups assert that the only answer to reduce marginalization of LGB and SSA students at Christian colleges and universities is to do away with the institutional policy against same-sex sexual practice. However, the researcher questioned whether this was the only answer. If Christian colleges and universities abandoned their position on same-sex sexual practice, would LGB students no longer feel marginalized? But if Christian colleges and universities maintained their positions on same-sex sexual practice, would LGB students continue to feel marginalized? The researcher struggled with the limitations of these two options and felt that the answer was more complex than simply the policies. The researcher was uncertain what another option might be. There was no research that focused on reducing marginalization of LGB students at Christian colleges and universities with few options for answers. Therefore, it was decided to seek input from the very ones who feel marginalized, LGB and SSA students, thus giving a voice to the voiceless. This study sought to discover other options for reducing marginalization of LGB and SSA students at Christian colleges and universities without changing policies that directly reflect the school's biblical foundation and religious identity. *Therefore, this is the first study of its kind and hopefully the beginning of more research and attention toward marginalization toward*

7. Monroe, "Back-to-School Not Welcoming."
8. Leighton, "Salem Nixes Gordon College Contract."
9. Ortega, "Lynn Public Schools Sever Relationship."

3

LGB and SSA students and the negative campus climate for these students at Christian colleges and universities.

Some of those who are decision makers and in positions of authority (e.g., trustees, presidents, vice presidents, deans, etc.) may wonder why there is even a need to reduce marginalization of LGB and SSA students. In addition to the biblical reasons that will be laid out in the following chapter, this study showed that many LGB and SSA students had no one to walk with or talk to them as they navigated issues of sexual identity. They struggled all alone, which sometimes resulted in seeking answers off campus from unbelievers, because they felt that there was no one else they could turn to. Although almost all the respondents began with a traditional view of sexuality (TVS), several ended up holding to a progressive view of sexuality (PVS). The researcher wonders how much of this was due to the respondents not sensing the freedom to process their struggles with other Christian friends on campus. It is difficult to share with others about experiencing unwanted same-sex attractions, but struggling alone is a far greater challenge.

God has provided the body of Christ so that Christians do not have to struggle alone in their pursuit of holiness and purity. The ideal context for sanctification to occur is in Christian community, not in isolation. The researcher is convinced that students are best supported if they are able to share their questions, fears, or struggles with trusted others in Christian community. The Enemy's best weapon is isolation. The best place for students to navigate through issues of sexual identity is in Christian community. As a matter of fact, Christian community should be the safest place in the world. And yet right now, our Christian college and university campuses are not perceived to be a healthy place for LGB and SSA students to be transparent. Trustees, presidents, vice presidents and deans should be proactive in making their campuses a safe *and redemptive* place for all of their students, including SSA students and students who identify as LGB.

Statement of the Research Problem

The problem this project addressed was the sense of marginalization experienced by LGB and SSA Christian college and university students. In response to this problem, the researcher: (1) carried out a biblical and theological study of issues related to compassion for the marginalized; (2) developed the research instrument, which was a mixed methods questionnaire focusing on the experiences of Christian college or university LGB and SSA students and on recommendations for Christian colleges and universities to become less marginalizing for LGB and SSA students; (3) obtained approval from the Institutional Review Board (IRB) before proceeding with the study; (4) recruited a minimum of thirty LGB or SSA Christian college or university students and alumni to complete the online questionnaire; (5) analyzed and evaluated the data from the online questionnaire; and (6) identified major themes from the data on the experiences of Christian college or university LGB and SSA students and on recommendations for Christian colleges and universities to become less marginalizing for LGB and SSA students.

Delimitations and Assumptions

The research was limited to Christian colleges and universities that held a TVS and had institutional policies prohibiting intimate sexual relations outside marriage between a husband and wife, including same-sex sexual practice. The research was limited to LGB and SSA people who were current students or recent alumni (within the past ten years) of Christian colleges and universities. The research was limited to the participants' experiences as LGB and SSA students and to their recommendations on how their Christian college or university can improve in helping LGB and SSA students feel less marginalized. This research was limited to how Christian colleges and universities can improve in making LGB and SSA students feel less marginalized.

This research did not focus on sexual identity development or formation. This research did not focus on challenging Christian colleges and universities to change their position on homosexuality from a TVS to a PVS. This research did not focus on the debate whether same-sex sexual practice and/or same-sex romantic relationships are sinful. This research did not focus upon transsexuality, transgenderism, gender identity disorder, or gender dysphoria. This research did not focus upon Title IX or future religious freedom implications for Christian institutions of higher education. This research did not focus on a critique of identifying as a lesbian, gay, or bisexual Christian. It only sought to accurately report how the respondents identified themselves without any assessment. Personally, the researcher finds the gay, lesbian, or bisexual identity label lacking (especially as it encompasses the sociological aspectof also identifying closer with that community than any other community) and has not found any label to be sufficient.[10]

The first assumption is that God had communicated to his people through the Bible and it is the final word and authority on faith and ethics. The second assumption is that the Bible has communicated that sexual intimacy is reserved for a husband and wife in marriage and anything outside of this is sinful, including same-sex sexual practice. The third assumption is that Christian colleges and universities should work to reduce the marginalization of LGB and SSA students.

Context of the Project

The United States has more than 4,700 degree-granting institutions of higher education. Among these institutions, 3,100 are private, nonprofit institutions, and 1,000 of these private institutions would define themselves as having religious affiliations. Although not all Christian colleges and universities require a Christian faith statement from their students, many Christian institutions require students to abide by their lifestyle agreement. Most lifestyle agreements prescribe that God has only reserved sexual activity for marriage between a husband and a wife. Thus, same-sex sexual practice (and often same-sex romantic relationships) is not permitted at these institutions, resulting in possible disciplinary action.

LGB and SSA students at Christian colleges and universities are often afraid to confide with others about their sexuality. Some LGB and SSA people do not gain enough courage until after graduation to disclose their sexual orientation. Yet, this is changing. A *New York Times* writer commented, "Decades after the gay rights movement swept the country's secular schools, more gays and lesbians at Christian colleges are starting to come out of the closet, demanding a right to proclaim their identities and form campus clubs, and rejecting suggestions to seek help in suppressing homosexual desires."[11] In the past few years, several gay alumni and student groups of Christian colleges and universities have formed. Although a few groups are officially sanctioned by their institutions, most are not. Additionally, many of these groups focus more upon advocacy than support. Their websites communicate that LGB students at their institutions feel

10. This is a good discussion on identity and sexuality: Butterfield, *Openness Unhindered.*

11. Eckholm, "Students Fight for Gay Identity."

alienated, ashamed, trapped, fearful, inauthentic, alone, depressed, sinful, shameful, isolated, and marginalized. The answer for many of these groups is that the institutional policies on homosexuality must change in order for LGB and SSA students to feel less marginalized.

Personal Context

When the researcher was around nine years old, he became aware of his attractions toward the same sex. Growing up, the researcher experienced marginalization for being different. Boys teased him for being Asian and for being effeminate, often calling him "sissy" and "fag." Although the teasing stopped in high school and college, the researcher still felt like an outsider and did not fit in to the expected social norms as other boys began dating girls. He came out of the closet in his early twenties as a graduate student pursuing a doctorate in dentistry. For more than six years, the researcher lived openly as a gay man while also selling illicit drugs. He was expelled from dental school and later arrested. In prison, the researcher became a Christian. After serving three years in federal prison, he was called to full-time vocational ministry and decided to attend Bible college.

At this institution, the researcher was in his thirties and much older than his other classmates. He was very open about his own sexuality and journey, and did not sense much marginalization. Yet, he knew that other LGB and SSA students felt marginalized as the campus climate did not seem to foster transparency among LGB and SSA students. He completed a master's degree and a doctorate of ministry at two separate Christian institutions. The researcher has had much firsthand experience as an SSA student, teacher, and speaker at Christian colleges and universities.

Prior to becoming a Christian, the researcher believed that same-sex relationships were not wrong, but good. Now, he holds to the traditional view of sexuality. Currently, the researcher speaks nationally and internationally on sexuality and Christian faith in churches, at conferences, and at close to fifty Christian colleges and universities. He has also been an adjunct instructor at a Bible college. Through his affiliations with so many different Christian colleges and universities, the researcher has had countless personal interactions with LGB and SSA students and alumni.

Importance of the Project

How the church responds to the topic of homosexuality will have untold ramifications. It is one of the most relevant and divisive issues of the day. The topic of homosexuality has divided government, media, public schools, and even churches. Some denominations are on the brink of splitting over the morality or immorality of same-sex sexual practice and romantic relationships (e.g., Anglican Communion) while others have openly affirmed same-sex unions (e.g., Evangelical Lutheran Church of America, Presbyterian Church USA).

Although conservative denominations maintain a traditional view of sexuality, few are addressing the marginalization of LGB and SSA people in their congregations. This research can help give a voice to LGB and SSA Christians who believe homosexual relationships are not blessed by God, but feel they cannot reveal their struggle to others. This research can also provide helpful steps on how the church can better minister to LGB and SSA people.

Philip Ryken, president of Wheaton College, believes that one of the three most significant theological issues that he is facing today is "human sexuality and a Christian understanding of marriage and sexual behavior."[12] There are many gay alumni advocacy groups of Christian colleges and universities claiming that LGB and SSA students are suffering harm on these campuses. The answer for these gay alumni advocacy groups is to eliminate the institutional policies against same-sex sexual practice. However, the researcher believes that these institutions can become less marginalizing for LGB and SSA students without changing their core values or institutional policies.

Nature of the Research

This project was both quantitative and qualitative in nature. Mixed methods methodology with an emphasis on phenomenology was the main methodology employed. The primary instrument for data collection was an online questionnaire.

12. Morgan, "Sailing into the Storm."

Data Required

Primary data included questionnaires from LGB and SSA people who were current students or recent alumni (within the past ten years) of Christian colleges and universities. The Christian colleges and universities that participated were determined after communicating with personal contacts that the researcher had developed over the past several years of speaking at Christian colleges and universities. Additionally, data was utilized from a pilot study on LGB and SSA students and alumni of a certain Christian college. Secondary data included Bible commentaries, books, journal articles, dissertations, and policies of Christian colleges and universities related to homosexuality (e.g., applications, student handbooks, community life policies, or other statements). Other secondary data consisted of online statements from LGBT alumni and student groups and personal stories from their websites.

$-$ 2 $-$

Biblical Reflection on Compassion
for the Marginalized

I N THIS CHAPTER, THE researcher carried out a biblical and theological study of issues related to compassion for the marginalized. The study was limited to biblical examples of the marginalized, developing a theology of compassion for the marginalized, and a comparison between the marginalized and LGB and SSA people.

Biblical Examples of the Marginalized

The Sojourner

One example of someone who was at risk of marginalization in the Bible was the sojourner. Sojourner (*gēr*) in the Old Testament has also been translated as stranger, alien, or foreigner. *Gēr* occurs ninety-two times in the Hebrew Bible, of which sixty-two occurrences are found in the Pentateuch. The root of this Hebrew word is from the verb "to dwell for a time"[1] or "to live among people who are not blood relatives."[2] Israel understood *gēr* to be a person who left one's land with or without family because of war, famine, or other reasons, such as to seek residence in another place. As a result, the rights of the sojourner (e.g., property rights, marriage rights, etc.) were restricted, placing the sojourner at risk of being oppressed and taken

1. Brown et al., *Hebrew and English Lexicon*, 158.
2. Stigers, "גּוּר (*gûr*)," 1:155.

advantage of. Therefore, the sojourner was in need of protection.[3] The *gēr* in Israel may have been considered a proselyte (LXX sometimes translates *gēr* as *prosēlytos* or proselyte, cf. Exod 12:48–49; 20:10, 20) and required to obey some of the laws that the native Israelites followed. A circumcised sojourner could participate in the Passover (Exod 12:48) and was expected to show the same fidelity to the Lord as a native Israelite.[4] Although the sojourner was a resident alien in Israel with conceded rights, these rights were not inherited and thus the sojourner was vulnerable and dependent upon the Israelite for protection.[5] There is some scholarly discussion on the definition of *gēr* in Deuteronomy, which occurs twenty-two times, more than any other Old Testament book. Most understand that *gēr* in Deuteronomy referred to a non-Israelite,[6] while a few believe *gēr* may refer to Israelites from the northern tribes who had migrated to Judah.[7] However, the latter view is more dependent on documentary hypothesis and on a largely monarchial reading of Deuteronomy. Thus this view is unlikely for those who read the Pentateuch and the rest of Scripture canonically. In addition, the plural form of *gēr* found in the Pentateuch (Exod 22:21; 23:9; Lev 19:34; 25:23; and Deut 10:19) referred exclusively to Israel as a whole and not merely to the northern tribes of Israel. Nevertheless, in the Old Testament, *gēr* was not a resident with inherited rights and therefore at risk of marginalization and oppression.

Several words were used in the New Testament to convey the concept of the sojourner. One of those words is *paroikos,* occurring four times in the New Testament (Acts 7:6, 29; Eph 2:19; 1 Pet 2:11) and is translated "sojourner," "stranger," "exile," "foreigner," or "alien" in the NIV, ESV, and NASB. In Acts 7, Stephen made a clear connection to the Old Testament with an allusion or quote from Genesis 15:13 and Exodus 2:15.[8] In Ephesians 2 and 1 Peter 2, Paul and Peter reminded first-century Christians that they were citizens in the household of God (*oikeioi tou theou*) and only sojourners of this world. Most likely, Peter was not referring to Christians

---

3. Köhler and Baumgartner, "גֵּר," 1:201.

4. Stigers, 156.

5. BDB, 158.

6. Begg, "Foreigner," 2:829; Mayes, *Deuteronomy,* 124–25; Ridderbos, *Deuteronomy,* 58, 175; van Houten, *The Alien in Israelite Law,* 107.

7. Kellerman, "גּוּר *gûr*," 2:445; Lohfink, "Poverty in the Laws," 41; Yan Yu, "The Alien in Deuteronomy," 113–14.

8. Schmidt et al., "πάροικος, παροικία, παροικέω," , 5:851.

sojourning "from this life to the next" as some have understood this passage, but rather referring to their "particular social status as people without rights and without a permanent residence in the Roman empire."[9] Whether their lower social status was a reality before conversion, a result of conversion, or a combination of both, it is certain that first-century Christians were socially excluded from power and privilege. They were more susceptible to oppression and had few options to seek justice from those in authority. As a result, Peter exhorted Christians to be particularly exemplary in their behavior even in the smallest of matters so that others could not persecute or accuse them of inappropriate behavior.[10]

Another word used in the New Testament to convey the concept of the sojourner was *parepidēmos*, which occurs three times in the New Testament (Heb 11:13; 1 Pet 1:1; 2:11). It is translated as "exile," "strangers," and "aliens" in the NIV, ESV, and NASB. In 1 Peter 1:1, the status of sojourner was the result of the diaspora. These elect (*eklektos*) had left their homes to live in a land where they did not belong. Although these elect sojourners (*eklektois parepidēmois*) were without inheritance or inheritable rights, Peter reminded them that they had an "inheritance that is imperishable, undefiled, and unfading, kept in heaven" (1 Pet 1:4).[11] Although they were grieved and faced many trials as elect sojourners, they were to rejoice that the genuineness of their faith was being tested, resulting "in praise and glory and honor at the revelation of Jesus Christ" (1 Pet 1:6-7).

The third word conveying the concept of sojourner was *xenos*. It occurred fourteen times in the New Testament (Matt 25:35, 38, 43–44; 27:7; Acts 17:18, 21; Rom 16:23; Eph 2:12, 19; Heb 11:13; 13:9; 1 Pet 4:12; and 3 John 1:5). This word is mostly translated as "stranger," "foreigner," or "alien" in the NIV, ESV, and NASB. There are four exceptions. In Acts 17:18, *xenōn* is translated as "foreign gods" or "strange deities." In Romans 16:23, *xenos* is translated as "host" or "hospitality." In Hebrews 13:9, *xenais* is translated as "strange teachings." In 1 Peter 4:12, *xenou* is translated "strange thing." The stem of this word, *xen-*, can be defined either as "strange" or as "guest" (e.g., the concept of hospitality, cf. *xenia, xenodocheō, philoxenia, philoxenos*).[12] On the surface, this tension between "strange" and "guest" appears to be

9. McKnight, *1 Peter*, 125.

10. McKnight, 125–26.

11. Unless otherwise noted, all Scripture citations are from *The Holy Bible, English Standard Version.*

12. Stählin, "ξένος, ξενία, ξενίζω, ξενοδοχέω, φιλοξενία, φιλόξενος," 5:1–2.

contradictory. The stranger was perceived by native Israelites as a possible threat. On the other hand, the stranger viewed the native Israelites as potentially dangerous. There was fear on both sides. The simple answer may be to dispose of this stranger. However, more problems could arise through revenge or retaliation. The solution was hospitality that transformed the "stranger" into a "guest." Hospitality and treating the stranger as a guest was an integral part of ancient Near Eastern societies.[13] Life and survival in the ancient Near Eastern world was dependent on the fusion of "strange" and "guest" in the form of hospitality toward the sojourner.

The Widow

Another example in the Bible of someone who was at risk of marginalization and oppression was the widow or 'almānā. This Hebrew word occurred fifty-five times in the Old Testament. For ancient Israelites, the 'almānā was simply "a wife whose husband [was] dead."[14] She was unimportant, powerless, and defenseless. Because her husband had died, the 'almānā was vulnerable to injustice and her husband's inheritance could be extorted rather easily. The 'almānā was often elderly, without income, and easy prey to the unscrupulous; thus, taking advantage of widows was viewed as an example of wickedness.[15] The widow did not have inheritance rights. In Numbers 27:8-11, the 'almānā was not listed as a possible recipient of a dead man's inheritance. The list is as follows in order: sons, daughters, brothers, father's brothers, nearest kinsmen of his clan.[16] The 'almānā was a woman who had "no obligated basis of support from the patrilineage of her husband and [had] limited economic resources at her disposal."[17]

> From these descriptions, the following points are clear: (1) sometimes the widow has no relative; (2) in some cases, there is a relative who is supposed to be responsible for her support and defense. However, it was also possible that the relative might regard her as too onerous an economic burden, and for that reason he might not help her. Moreover, the widow's relative might not want

13. Stählin, "ξένος," 2–4.

14. Köhler and Baumgartner, "אַלְמָנָה," 1:58.

15. Scott, "אַלְמָנָה ('almānā)," in Theological Wordbook of the Old Testament, 1:47.

16. Van Leeuwen, "אַלְמָנָה," 1:413.

17. Steinberg, "Romancing the Widow," 1:328.

any connection with her, because she was regarded as an inferior element in society.[18]

With little protection, the 'almānā was dangerously disadvantaged "because it left her economically vulnerable to oppression from those who wished to take her land if she had no offspring or if they were too young to inherit directly."[19] John Rook makes the argument that a woman became an 'almānā not "when her husband dies, but when she has no male guardian from the kin group to look out for her interests."[20] For Rook, an 'almānā was a woman who did not have any male support or protection.[21] For a woman in ancient Near Eastern times, this was not only dangerous but could be life threatening.

Similar to the Old Testament, the New Testament often mentioned the widow (chēra) with the orphan. Chēra occurs twenty-six times in the New Testament and has a close association to the idea of neediness.[22] It is related to words like chēroō, which means "to make desolate, forsake," and chēra is the root of the adjective chēros, which means "deprived, bereaved, widowed."[23] During biblical times, widowhood was a state most feared by women, especially in the pagan cultures. If her husband died, the widow could only return to her own family if the dowry was paid back to the husband's heirs. Otherwise the widow must stay with her husband's family and "took an even more subordinate and often humiliating position . . . [and often] was not allowed to remarry." Therefore at their husband's burial, women often chose death over living the marginalized and defenseless position of a widow.[24]

Jesus had deep compassion for the widow. Luke's Gospel in particular had an interest in widows, which fit into Luke's broader emphasis on the marginalized, oppressed, and despised, especially the women and the poor.[25] In 1 Timothy 5:3, Paul made a distinction of a true widow (ontō chēra): "Honor widows who are truly widows." During the first century, life was short and men often died at an early age, leaving behind young

18. Galpaz-Feller, "The Widow in the Bible," 233.

19. Mayes, "The Resident Alien," 62.

20. Rook, "Making Widows," 10–15.

21. Rook, "When Is a Widow Not a Widow?" 4–6.

22. Bauer et al., Greek-English Lexicon, 1084.

23. Silva, NIDNTTE, 4:668.

24. Stählin, "χήρα," 9:441–42.

25. Stählin, "χήρα," 450.

widows. A few of these widows may actually have been wealthy, and for Paul, these self-sufficient widows would not have been considered "true widows."[26] Paul provided three criteria for a "true widow" (*ontōs chēra*). First, she was "not less than sixty years of age" (1 Tim 5:9a). Second, she must have been "the wife of one husband" (1 Tim 5:9b). Third, she had "a reputation for good works" (1 Tim 5:10). In 1 Timothy 5:3, the verb "honor" is in the imperative mood. Therefore, Paul commanded Christians to honor and care for "true widows" not only as an affirmation of the Old Testament teaching on widows, but also as a strong witness to unbelievers of how Christians cared for the marginalized and needy.[27]

The Orphan

In the Old Testament, "orphan" (*yāttôm*) occurs forty-two times. There is general consensus that *yāttôm* denotes a fatherless child.[28] Mayes points out that "motherless" should not be disregarded as a possible meaning; however, its usage in context must be taken into consideration.[29] Moreover, in the Greek Septuagint, the Hebrew word for "orphan" (*yāttôm*) was translated into *orphanos,* and in classical Greek this meant "bereaved" or "without parents."[30] Like the Hebrew concept of orphan, *orphanos* sometimes referred to a child who lost only one parent (e.g., in Homer's classical Greek texts).[31] There are only two occurrences of *orphanos* in the New Testament (John 14:18; Jas 1:27). In John 14:18, Jesus said, "I will not leave you as orphans; I will come to you." This figurative use of *orphanos* refers to "being without the aid and comfort of one who serves as associate and friend."[32] It is similar to Plato's figurative use of *orphanos* describing the pupils of Socrates who were left behind by their teacher, feeling completely orphaned and bereaved.[33] The second instance of *orphanos* is in James 1:27:

26. Liefeld, *1 and 2 Timothy, Titus*, 175.

27. Liefeld, 179.

28. BDB, 450; Hamilton, "יָתוֹם," 2:570–71; Hartley, "יתם (*ytm*)," 1:419; Holwerda and Harrison, "Orphan," 3:616–17; Köhler and Baumgartner, "יָתוֹם," 1:451; Ringgren, "יָתוֹם *yāttôm*," 6:479.

29. Mayes, "Resident Alien," 63.

30. Seesemann, "ὀρφανός," 5:487.

31. BDAG, 725.

32. BDAG, 725.

33. Seesemann, 488.

"Religion that is pure and undefiled before God, the Father, is this: to visit orphans and widows in their affliction." James was heavily influenced by the Old Testament and reiterated a common demand found in the Hebrew Scriptures to care for orphans and widows (cf. Exod 22:21; Deut 24:17). This was the only admonition to care for orphans found in the New Testament and the earliest admonition in Christian literature with many similar exhortations in Christian writings after the New Testament.[34]

Why was the orphan (*yāttôm*) in danger of marginalization? Like the *'almānā*, the *yāttôm* shared a similar vulnerable, lower sociological position. Of the forty-two occurrences of *yāttôm* in the Old Testament, thirty-two had a direct or indirect reference to *'almānā*. This implies that the fatherless and the widow shared analogous challenges that male citizens of the land did not experience. The fatherless and widow were powerless and did not have any part in the ruling patriarchy. Although a fatherless child could be in line as an heir to inherit the land of the family, this posed a threat to others who were in succession as well. The *yāttôm* was at risk of being defrauded through some judicial maneuvering, unless the child was protected by a male relative.[35] The Old Testament portrayed widowhood and being fatherless as a curse or punishment (cf. Exod 22:24; Ps 109:9). Yet the people of Israel were commanded to extend justice to the *yāttôm* and the *'almānā* (Deut 24:17) for the Lord himself was their defender and provider (Deut 10:18). This special concern that the Lord had for the *yāttôm* is endearingly expressed in the powerful statement that God is a "father to the fatherless" (Ps 68:5).

In summary, the sojourner, the widow, and the orphan were examples of marginalized people in the Bible who were socially outcast, unimportant, and powerless. Sojourners were marginalized and at risk of oppression because they had no inherited rights. Not only were sojourners without tangible rights, but also they were socially disadvantaged and sometimes viewed as a threat, thus very dependent upon the kindness and hospitality of native residents in order to survive. Widows were marginalized and at risk of oppression because they were without adult male support or protection after their husband's death. Even though the widow was to be cared for by her husband's family, she was often viewed as a liability and would hold a rather humiliating position in her husband's family as a result (cf. Tamar in Genesis 38). Orphans were marginalized

34. Seesemann, 488.
35. Mayes, "Resident Alien," 63–64.

and at risk of oppression because, like widows, they were without adult male support or protection. Although possibly in line as a recipient to the family's inheritance, the orphan could easily lose his birthright without adult male protection. Therefore, Israelites and Christians were admonished to care for marginalized widows and orphans as an example of "pure and undefiled" religion (Jas 1:27; cf. Isaiah 58).

Developing a Theology of Compassion for the Marginalized

Isaiah prophesied to the nation of Judah, which had become rebellious and corrupt. Their rebellion resulted in Judah's desolation at the hand of God with more to follow.[36] However, the people of Judah believed that if they were only more strict in following ritualism and formal religion, God would relent of the impending judgment and actually bless them. God scoffed at their response of shallow ritualism (Isa 1:11–15). The Lord had enough of their sacrifices and took no pleasure in them (Isa 1:11). A double entendre was most likely intended in Isaiah 1:15: "Your hands are full of blood." Not only were their hands full of the blood of sacrifices, but also their hands were full of the blood of the innocent they had abused.[37] The Lord desired Judah to "learn to do good; seek justice, correct oppression; bring justice to the fatherless, plead the widow's cause" (Isa 1:17). Their formal or false religion was at the expense of compassion and human relationships. True religion integrates the formal (truth) and relational (grace) aspects of religion without the expense of either.[38] Isaiah returned to this important point in chapter 58 when he expressed his reproach toward Judah's self-centered fasting.

> Is not this the fast that I choose:
> to loose the bonds of wickedness,
> to undo the straps of the yoke,
> to let the oppressed go free,
> and to break every yoke?
> Is it not to share your bread with the hungry
> and bring the homeless poor into your house;
> when you see the naked, to cover him,
> and not to hide yourself from your own flesh? (Isa 58:6-7)

36. Oswalt, *Isaiah*, 59.

37. Oswalt, *Isaiah*, 64–65.

38. Oswalt, *Book of Isaiah*, 494.

True religion should result in having compassion for the marginalized. Yet, true religion is not merely having compassion for the marginalized, nor is it merely fasting and obeying the Sabbath. The more important issue at stake is finding delight in the Lord (Isa 58:14) as opposed to focusing on seeking to please oneself (cf. Isa 58:3, 13).[39] There must not be a dichotomy between external religion (i.e., fasting, obeying the Sabbath) and internal religion (i.e., delighting in the Lord). "What pleases God is the combination of both, when his nature has become so much a part of a person's being that worship expresses a love for God which is so deep that it must overflow in compassion and love for others, especially those weaker."[40]

This deep connection between loving God and having compassion for others was made even more evident in the life of Jesus. When Jesus was asked which was the greatest commandment, he responded with a twofold answer (Matt 22:37–39; Mark 12:29–31). The greatest commandment was to love God (Deut 6:5) and the second commandment was to love one's own neighbor (Lev 19:18). But there is a connection that links the second greatest commandment with the call to compassion for the marginalized, a connection that is often missed. Jesus reiterated that his followers were to love their neighbors "as yourself." Jesus was referring to Leviticus 19:18, and apart from this passage, there was only one other time in the Old Testament where God commanded Israel to love someone or something "as yourself." In Leviticus 19:34, Moses wrote, "You shall treat the stranger who sojourns with you as the native among you, and you shall love him as yourself, for you were strangers in the land of Egypt: I am the Lord your God." With Jesus proclaiming the second commandment to "love your neighbor as yourself," it would be difficult to ignore its similar passage to love the stranger "as yourself." This connection may very well cast light on the broader social implications of neighbor love.

With his simple and concise answer of loving God and loving neighbor, Jesus summed up "all the Law and the Prophets" (Matt 22:40). This double answer brought together the two aspects of Christian ministry: proclamation and social justice. Sadly, one is sometimes overemphasized at the expense of the other. And yet for Jesus, these two options were not mutually exclusive[41], and he warned not to neglect one or the other (Luke 11:42). When Jesus was anointed at Bethany, saying "For you always have

---

39. Oswalt, *Book of Isaiah*, 494.

40. Oswalt, *Book of Isaiah*, 502.

41. Bruner, *Matthew: A Commentary*, 414.

the poor with you, but you will not always have me" (Matt 26:6-13; cf. Mark 14:3-9; John 12:1-8), he protected "divine worship from a progressive or people-centered usurpation."[42] Unfortunately, this one-sided focus would be an example of loving one's neighbor at the expense of loving God.

Isaiah, Micah, and James warned of the other extreme of loving God at the expense of loving one's own neighbor, or at least the futile, human attempts at this. The prophet Isaiah wrote: "I have had enough of burnt offerings of rams and the fat of well-fed beasts; I do not delight in the blood of bulls, or of lambs, or of goats. . . . [Rather] learn to do good; seek justice, correct oppression; bring justice to the fatherless, plead the widow's cause" (Isa 1:11, 17). "Is not this the fast that I choose: to loose the bonds of wickedness, to undo the straps of the yoke, to let the oppressed go free, and to break every yoke?" (Isa 58:6). Micah also wrote: "He has told you, O man, what is good; and what does the Lord require of you but to do justice, and to love kindness, and to walk humbly with your God?" (Micah 6:8). This teaching found in the Old Testament is also in the New Testament. James writes: "Religion that God our Father accepts as pure and faultless is this: to look after orphans and widows in their distress and to keep oneself from being polluted by the world" (Jas 1:27). These two commandments must not be independent from one another. Rather, love for God is the best place for people to begin their love for people.[43] For Chrysostom and Calvin, loving one's neighbor flowed from loving God first. The power of the second commandment to love one's neighbor derives from the first and greatest commandment to love God.[44]

Not only is there a correlation between loving God and having compassion for others, but also, when one cares for the marginalized, it is equivalent to caring for Jesus himself. Jesus said in Matthew 25:40, "Truly, I say to you, as you did it to one of the least of these my brothers, you did it to me." Not only does the one being helped represent Jesus, but also the one being helped *is* Jesus.[45] The general principle from Proverbs 19:17a, "Whoever is generous to the poor lends to the Lord," was applied to Jesus and affirmed as a critical mandate in the lives of God's people. Jesus had compassion for the marginalized, and likewise, his followers must minister

42. Ibid., 413.

43. Bruner, 413–14.

44. Chrysostom, *Homilies on Saint Matthew*, 431; Calvin, *Commentary on a Harmony*, 3:59.

45. France, *Matthew*, 964.

in the same way.[46] Scholars differ on how best to interpret the attribution "brothers" in Matthew 25:40. "Brothers" can refer to (1) Christ's disciples in need;[47] (2) a Christian in need;[48] or (3) generally any person in need.[49] All three focus upon people in need, but the third option (any person in need) is more consistent to Jesus' teachings in the Gospels. As Davies and Allison rightly pointed out, there are no qualifications to Jesus' statement, "Blessed are the merciful, for they shall receive mercy" (Matt 5:7). "Is not the identification of the needy with all in distress more consistent with the command to ignore distinctions between insiders and outsiders and with Jesus' injunction to love even enemies?"[50] Caring for anyone who is needy and marginalized is caring for Jesus.

The biblical writers in the Old Testament and New Testament provided many examples of the religious being reticent to care for the marginalized. In Luke 10:25–37, a lawyer or expert in the Mosaic Law tested Jesus: "What shall I do to inherit eternal life?" Jesus answered the questions with his own questions: "What is written in the Law? How do you read it?"[51] It was likely that the lawyer had previously heard Jesus expounding on the double love commandment and intentionally repeated it as a segue to his follow-up question, "Who is my neighbor?"[52] The lawyer wanted to "justify himself" (Luke 10:29) by minimizing the scope of responsibility and obedience required of him.[53] He wanted to know who was *not* his neighbor in order to limit those whom he needed to love. Unfazed, Jesus delivered the well-known Good Samaritan parable and concluded with a counter-question: "Which of these three, do you think, proved to be a neighbor to the man who fell among the robbers?" (Luke 10:36). Jesus is a master storyteller and, as he so often does, turns stories on their head to make a bold and provocative point. Most miss this unexpected twist. Jesus' question was completely unexpected because it was a reversal of what most would expect. The predictable question would have been: "Which of these

46. Morris, *Matthew*, 639.

47. France, 964–65; Morris, *Matthew*, 639.

48. Gray, "The Least of My Brothers," , 358.

49. Blomberg, *Matthew*, 377–78; Davies and Allison, *Commentary on Matthew*, 3:429.

50. Davies and Allison, 429.

51. Bock, *Luke: 9:51–24:53*, 1024.

52. Stein, *Luke*, 315.

53. Bock, 1028.

three, do you think, treated the man who fell among the robbers *as his neighbor?*" Since the man who fell among robbers was in desperate need, it would seem natural that the person in need of love should be viewed as the neighbor. In a massive reversal of roles, the person in need was not the neighbor, but the neighbor was the Samaritan.

The purpose of this rhetorical strategy was twofold. First, Jews regarded Samaritans as unclean and among the least respected people. Even eating with them was equivalent to eating pork.[54] This hostility between Jews and Samaritans could be traced back to the rebuilding of the temple (Ezra 4–6; Nehemiah 2–4).[55] Jesus intentionally inserted the Samaritan to communicate that "the love of one's neighbor must transcend all natural or human boundaries such as race, nationality, religion and economic or educational status."[56] Sexuality could also be added to this list. Loving one's neighbor means loving those who may be different from the majority and from those deemed undeserving of love. It means loving the unlovable for "neighbor love knows no boundaries."[57]

The second point may be the most important and most overlooked. The parable of the Good Samaritan is often understood as an exhortation to be *like the Good Samaritan,* showing deep compassion for the needy. And since the neighbor was the Samaritan, many commentators explain that this was a call to *be* a good neighbor.[58] However, the parable began with the lawyer's answer to love "your neighbor as yourself" (Luke 10:27) and the lawyer's question, "Who is my neighbor?" Was the answer Jesus gave, "Be a good neighbor"? This was unlikely. A call to *be* a good neighbor would seem to emphasize one's own good works (anthropocentric) and less upon God's grace and the gospel (Christocentric). Therefore, the lawyer was not called to *be* like the Good Samaritan. He was called to *love* the Good Samaritan. And the only character in the parable capable of loving the Samaritan was the nameless man who fell among the robbers. How could this be? Imagine the man coming back to consciousness and the innkeeper explaining that it was a Samaritan man who bound his wounds, brought him to the inn, and promised to pay for his recovery. Would this man now have extravagant

54. Bock, 1031.

55. Stein, *Luke,* 318.

56. Green, *Luke,* 426.

57. Green, 426.

58. Bock, 1018, 1034; Stein, *Luke,* 318; Green, 432; Morris, *Luke,* 208; Marshall, *Luke,* 450.

love for this Samaritan who saved his life? This love was not from his own good nature and was not according to societal norms. Rather, this love was overflowing from a grateful heart. In an unexpected twist of the story, Jesus subtly communicated that the only way one can love the unlovable, a Jew can love a Samaritan, and a Christian can love one's neighbor, was to realize that each person is really like the man who fell among the robbers. Because of sin, every person has been beaten and left half dead at the side of the road. But a Savior came and had compassion. A Savior even paid the price of his own life so that all humanity can be healed. It is only when one finds solidarity with the man who fell among the robbers, and believes in the Savior who showed compassion, that one is able to "love your neighbor as yourself." The main take away of this parable is not "Love your neighbor by being like the Good Samaritan," but rather it is "Love your neighbor because Jesus saved and loved you first."

Before John Calvin, most approached this parable allegorically and viewed the man who fell among the robbers to represent Adam or all of humanity (e.g., by Origen, Augustine, and Martin Luther).[59] Although the allegorical method may have been applied too liberally to every aspect of this parable, the possibility of finding solidarity with the man who fell among the robbers should not be so quickly dismissed with the other allegorical comparisons. If this had been a true story and not a parable, it is very likely that after recovering from his near-death experience, the man who fell among robbers would have been a completely different person. After being told that someone saved him and even paid the price for him to get well, he would certainly have *become* a grateful man. And with a new lease on life, any person he would meet would more readily *become* his neighbor. This is not out of a person's own goodness, but out of sincere gratefulness that someone showed him compassion first. The Samaritan can be viewed as a Christ-figure, and Christ showed the greatest compassion by even paying the price with his life so that sinners who believed in him would live.[60] He did this for the weak, for sinners, and even for God's enemies (Rom 5:6-10). Jesus exhorted his disciples at the Last Supper: "Just as I have loved you, you also are to love one another" (John 13:34). Loving God and loving one's neighbor must be the mark of a Christ follower. And one's neighbor should

59. Stein, *Introduction to the Parables*, 43–49.

60. Many before Martin Luther believed the Samaritan represented Christ, e.g., Clement of Alexandria (150–215), Origen (185–254), Basil (330–379), Cyril (313–386), Chrysostom (347–407), Augustine (354–430), Gregory the Great (540–604), Thomas Aquinas (1225–1274), Martin Luther (1483–1546). From Stein, *Parables*, 44–49.

never be narrowly defined, but "basic mercy and love is to extend to all."[61] The consequence of a radical love for God is a radical response to love one's neighbor.[62] Jesus does not require minimal or partial obedience, but total and radical obedience.

Remembering one's neediness was the Lord's way of cultivating in the lives of Israelites compassion for the marginalized. "You shall not pervert the justice due to the sojourner or to the fatherless, or take a widow's garment in pledge, but you shall remember that you were a slave in Egypt and the Lord your God redeemed you from there; therefore I command you to do this" (Deut 24:17-18; cf. Deut 15:15; 24:22). The way Israel was treated in Egypt was similar to the way that the man who fell among the robbers was treated. They were cruelly oppressed and physically abused. And just as the Samaritan delivered the man who fell among the robbers through acts of mercy and compassion, the Lord delivered Israel by his redemptive grace and power.[63] Moses sought "to motivate rather than legislate generosity by linking the well-being of the nation to their generosity to the marginalized . . . by remembering their own experience as slaves in Egypt."[64] As Israel executed justice toward the disadvantaged, this emulated the character of the Lord (Deut 10:18–19). Sympathy for the marginalized was not enough. Rather since God had "loved them, freed them, and made ample provisions for them . . . they should do no less."[65] Memory of and gratitude for God's grace are essential to a practical theology of compassion for the marginalized, even LGB and SSA people. For the people of Israel "were not simply being charitable to those less fortunate than themselves, they were expressing their gratitude to God, who had brought them out of the slavery in Egypt."[66]

The Marginalized and LGB and SSA People

There are parallels that can be drawn between the marginalized in the Bible and LGB and SSA people, though as with most comparisons, there are both similarities and differences. As the sojourner was excluded from

61. Bock, 1018.

62. Bock, 1035; Green, 426.

63. Merrill, *Deuteronomy*, 246.

64. Block, *Deuteronomy*, 572, cf. 372.

65. Craigie, *Deuteronomy*, 239.

66. Craigie, 311.

privilege as an outsider, likewise LGB and SSA people experience alienation for being different and not fitting in to a culture that is predominantly heterosexual. The foreigner and LGB and SSA person are often at risk of being mistreated and taken advantage of. LGB and SSA youth frequently experience verbal and physical abuse by their heterosexual peers, with few who are willing to stand up and protect them. Similar to the sojourner, LGB and SSA people find themselves in a vulnerable, lower social status and susceptible to oppression. The widow in the Old and New Testaments was unimportant, powerless, and defenseless. Similarly, the LGB and SSA person is vulnerable to injustice. Like the widow, LGB and SSA people are sometimes viewed as a liability by their own families. LGB and SSA people occasionally experience tension and rupture in their familial relationships because of their sexuality and therefore lose the protection and support of their own families. A 2006 study reported that 26 percent of gay teens were kicked out of their homes when they came out of the closet to their parents. In addition, 20 percent to 40 percent of all homeless youth are LGBT, compared to the 3 percent to 5 percent national average of LGBT people in the general population.[67] According to these statistics, there is a higher percentage of homeless LGB and SSA youth, many of them living, in essence, fatherless and motherless.

Although there are some similarities, there is a significant difference between comparing the sojourner, the widow, and the orphan and LGB and SSA people. This distinction is sinful behavior. Specifically, there is no sinful behavior uniquely associated with being a sojourner, a widow, or an orphan. Scripture does not condemn any specific sojourner behavior, widow behavior, or orphan behavior. However, those who hold to the traditional view of sexuality believe that the Bible does regard same-sex sexual practice as sinful. If sinful, then would God have compassion upon the one engaging in same-sex sexual practice? The Bible communicates that God who is just and righteous extends his wrath against all unrighteousness (Deut 32:4; Ps 7:11; 11:7; Rom 1:18). God is far from the wicked because sin separates the sinner from God, who does not answer the prayers of evildoers (Prov 15:29; Isa 59:2; Micah 3:4). Sin is an abomination in God's eyes, and in the strongest of words, God even hates, destroys, and abhors evildoers (Prov 6:16–19; Ps 5:5–6).

Nevertheless, God certainly has great concern and compassion for the sinner. This is the tension found in Scripture between God's wrath and

67. Ray, "Lesbian, Gay, Bisexual and Transgender Youth."

God's grace. Grace is foundational to understanding the basic tenets of the Christian faith. Grace can be defined as "God in his sovereign goodness entering human history and showering sinful creatures with undeserved favor."[68] The concept of grace is communicated throughout Scripture and "a proper consideration of grace is impossible without regard to the contextual issue of sin."[69] In contrast to saving grace, common grace is extended to all people, believers and unbelievers alike. This demonstrates God's goodness and mercy "in the blessings he gives to undeserving sinners."[70] David wrote in Psalm 145:9: "The Lord is good to all, and his mercy is over all that he has made." God's goodness and mercy is indiscriminately extended to all people of God's creation. The Apostle Paul quoted from Psalm 32:1–2, "Blessed are those whose lawless deeds are forgiven, and whose sins are covered; blessed is the man against whom the Lord will not count his sin," and commented, "Is this blessing then only for the circumcised, or also for the uncircumcised?" (Rom 4:7–9). God also spoke through the prophet Ezekiel: "As I live, declares the Lord God, I have no pleasure in the death of the wicked, but that the wicked turn from his way and live" (Ezek 33:11; cf. Ezek 18:21–23, 32). The Hebrew word for "turn" (*šwḇ*) an also be rendered "repent."[71] Even though the wicked deserve God's wrath, God does not delight in their punishment but would rather see the wicked repent and live. In the New Testament, Paul wrote to Timothy that God "desires all people to be saved and to come to the knowledge of the truth" (1 Tim 2:4). Therefore, God's grace and his just wrath are not diminished when sinners are shown compassion. Below are several examples in Scripture of sinners being shown compassion by God.

Before entering the Promised Land, the Lord reminded Israel to obey his commandments (Deut 26:16–19), since obedience would lead to life while disobedience would lead to death (Deut 30:15–20). In spite of Israel's disobedience, God continued to have compassion on this sinful and rebellious nation. The psalmist wrote that God would "redeem Israel from all his iniquities" (Ps 130:8) and in David's words, "He does not deal with us according to our sins, nor repay us according to our iniquities. . . . As far as the east is from the west, so far does he remove our transgressions from us" (Ps 103:10, 12). One may expect the Lord to have compassion on sinful

---

68. Demarest, *Cross and Salvation*, 49.

69. Demarest, 49.

70. Grudem, *Systematic Theology*, 657, 664.

71. Köhler and Baumgartner, "שׁוב," 2:1427.

Israel because they are *his* chosen people. But God also extended mercy to sinful Gentiles in the Old Testament. God called Jonah to preach to the people of Nineveh, the capital of Assyria. In the ancient Near East, the Assyrians were infamous for their unimaginable cruelty and violent brutality.[72] Even though the Ninevites were wicked and sinful Gentiles, God had compassion and relented from destroying that great city in Jonah 3. This undeserved compassion toward heathen was difficult for post-exilic Jews to accept, resulting in enduring theological dialogue concerning the propriety of the book of Jonah in the Hebrew canon.[73]

Like the Old Testament, the New Testament provided examples of compassion for sinners. Jesus, who ate with sinners (Matt 9:11; Mark 2:16; Luke 5:30, 15:2, 19:7), was accused of being a friend of sinners (Matt 11:19; Luke 7:34). Jesus articulated that he "came not to call the righteous, but sinners" (Matt 9:13b; Mark 2:17b; cf. Luke 5:32). In response to the Pharisees and the scribes who grumbled over his concern for sinners, Jesus delivered three parables about a lost sheep, a lost coin, and a lost son (Luke 15). The three parables communicated the joy that would occur in heaven when one sinner repents. The grumbling older brother served as a foil to indict those who had no compassion toward sinners. In the scandalous encounter between Jesus and the Samaritan woman in John 4, Jesus not only broke through social and gender boundaries, but also willingly and knowingly interacted with someone of "questionable moral character."[74] The Samaritan woman did not deny that she was living in sin with a man who was not her husband (John 4:17–19, 39). But Jesus did not condemn her on the spot. Instead, he offered her living water from which she would "never be thirsty" (John 4:14). Jesus also exemplified the prayer of a tax collector who beat his breast and said, "God, be merciful to me, a sinner!" (Luke 18:13). Although repentance may have been a common thread in these examples of compassion toward sinners, Paul reminded the church at Rome that God's kindness leads to and thus precedes repentance (Rom 2:4). And the greatest display of God's compassion is that while people were sinners and enemies of God, he showed his love by sending his son (Rom 5:8, 10). Although God is clearly just and righteous, he also has deep concern and compassion even for the sinner.

---

72. Bruckner, *Jonah, Nahum, Habakkuk, Zephaniah*, 17–19.

73. Ewert, *General Introduction to the Bible*, 71; Bruckner, 15.

74. Burge, *John*, 139.

Showing compassion toward unbelieving sinners is evidenced in Scripture; however, some would argue that professing Christians mired in unrepentant sin (e.g., same-sex sexual practice) must be treated differently. This is true, but even in instances of church discipline the goal must be restoration of the Christian sister or brother. In 1 Corinthians 5:11, Paul gave an exhortation not to eat with the sexually immoral "who bears the name of brother." This referred to a hedonistic and libertine man in the church of Corinth who was flaunting his freedom in Christ. What made things worse was that the church at Corinth refused to monitor and discipline the sinning Christian.[75] The offender in this situation was not one who simply lapsed into sinful behavior, but he was characterized by this sin and unrepentantly continuing in this sinful practice.[76] "Christians are identifiable by their conduct, not simply by their doctrine or verbal professions. If anyone goes by the name 'Christian' and is guilty of these sins, he or she is to be ostracized."[77] Therefore, the question remains, what does this ostracism look like? A main theme throughout 1 Corinthians is the community of believers and how they should act when together. Particularly in chapter 11, Paul wrote about eating the Lord's Supper when they come together in worship. It is likely that Paul's concern was not individual Christians dissociating from the sinning Christian, but rather that this person was "excluded from the community as it gathers for worship and instruction."[78] "To deliver this man to Satan" (1 Cor 5:5) meant to expel the man out of the church and into the realm where Satan reigns.[79] But even this exclusion from worship and eating at the Lord's Table should not be without a purpose. The purpose is the restoration of the sinning and unrepentant one. Although 2 Corinthians 2:5–11 most likely does not refer to the situation of the unrepentant brother in 1 Corinthians 5:11,[80] the importance of restoration is consistent with the writings of other New Testament authors (Matt 18:15–17; Gal 6:1; Jas 5:19–20). Excluding an unrepentant brother

---

75. Blomberg, *1 Corinthians*, 104.

76. Thiselton, *First Epistle to the Corinthians*, 413.

77. Garland, *1 Corinthians*, 187–88.

78. Fee, *First Epistle to the Corinthians*, 226.

79. Garland, *2 Corinthians*, 122.

80. Majority of ancient commentators believed that Paul was referring back to 1 Cor 5:11; however, the majority of modern commentators reject this. For more: Garland, *2 Corinthians*, 118–20.

or sister from worship gatherings must be implemented with the hope and intent of restoration.

Although a traditional view of sexuality maintains that same-sex sexual practice is sinful, same-sex temptation is not sin *per se*. However, it certainly quickly leads to sin (Jas 1:14–15). The writer of Hebrews made a distinction between temptation and sin: "For we do not have a high priest who is unable to sympathize with our weaknesses, but one who in every respect has been tempted as we are, yet without sin" (Heb 4:15). "Weakness" or *astheneia* is associated with having a "propensity to sin" (cf. Heb 4:15). In James 1:14–15, there is a progression from one's own desire to temptation, to sin, and finally to death. "James implies that temptation, in and of itself, is not sinful. Only when desire 'conceives'—is allowed to produce offspring—does sin come into being."[81] The evocative imagery of fishing or trapping is employed to refer to people being drawn out and baited by their own desire or evil capacity.[82] While the Greek word for desire in the New Testament often occurs in the plural when referring to sexual passions, desire in the singular suggests something more systemic. Borrowing from the concept of evil impulse (*yeser hara*) in rabbinic literature, James's use of desire is likely a person's innate tendency toward sin.[83]

There is debate among Christians who hold to the traditional view of sexuality whether same-sex attraction is sinful. A main reason for this confusion is due to the ambiguity of the exact meaning of "attraction" and how this overlaps with the biblical categories of sin and temptation. Attraction has a broad semantic range, which includes temptation, desire, and lust. The mistake is often made to equate same-sex attraction with same-sex temptation. The two are not the same. Same-sex temptation may be a subset of the broader category of same-sex attraction. However, same-sex temptation is not the same as same-sex attraction. Although, same-sex temptation is not sin *per se*, it is not neutral nor is it innocent.[84] It is a stark reality of the distorting effects of original sin. As a matter of fact, everyone's sexuality has been distorted post-Fall. Temptation can lead to sin, which can lead to death. Yet resisting, fighting, and fleeing temptation is a vital part of a mature Christian's life. The Puritan John Owen wrote, "Temptation is like a

---

81. Moo, *Letter of James*, 76.

82. McCartney, *James*, 106.

83. Moo, *James*, 73.

84. Butterfield, *Openness Unhindered*, 76.

knife, that may either cut the meat or the throat of a man; it may be his food or his poison, his exercise or his destruction."[85]

In conclusion, this chapter has carried out a biblical and theological study of issues related to compassion for the marginalized. The first principle is that there are clear examples of the marginalized found in the Bible. The second principle is that God calls his people to have compassion for the marginalized. The third principle is that there are similarities and dissimilarities found between the marginalized in the Bible and LGB and SSA people. Whereas LGB and SSA people not involved in same-sex sexual practice may more resemble the sojourner, the widow, and the orphan mentioned in the Bible, there is biblical evidence for the people of God to extend compassion and kindness even toward LGB and SSA people who may continue to be involved in unrepentant same-sex sexual practice.

85. Owen, *Overcoming Sin*, 152.

—— 3 ——

Project Description and Research Methods

I N THIS CHAPTER, THE researcher reviewed the project description and research methods. The first section provided background and support for the study design and research method. The researcher chose mixed methods as the appropriate methodology. The second section explained the research instrument and data collection procedures. The research instrument was a mixed methods questionnaire focusing on the experiences of Christian college or university LGB and SSA students and on recommendations for Christian colleges and universities to become less marginalizing for LGB and SSA students. The researcher obtained approval from the Institutional Review Board (IRB) before proceeding with the study. The data collection procedures included recruiting a minimum of thirty LGB or SSA Christian college or university students and alumni to complete the online questionnaire The third section reviewed the data analysis methodology.

Study Design and Research Method

To choose a study design and research method that would best fit a research project, the research question must be determined, for "the research question dictates the selection of research methods."[1] However, simply determining the research question was not sufficient. The researcher also had to ascertain the purpose behind the question to assist in identifying an appropriate method. Isadore Newman and colleagues asserted "by considering

1. Newman et al., "A Typology of Research Purposes," 170.

the question and purpose iteratively, one can eventually get to a design or set of designs that more clearly reflect the intent of the question."[2] John Creswell and Vicki Plano Clark state that the study design must be matched to the research problem, purpose, and questions.[3]

The problem this project addressed was the sense of marginalization experienced by LGB and SSA Christian college and university students. The purpose of the research was to gain information about how to reduce marginalization of LGB and SSA students at Christian colleges and universities. There were two research questions. The first research question was: What are the experiences of Christian college or university LGB and SSA students? The second research question was: How can the campus climate at Christian colleges and universities be less marginalizing for LGB and SSA students?

The research problem, purpose, and questions of this project lent to a study design that was primarily qualitative. Qualitative research is "a research paradigm designed to address questions of meaning, interpretation, and socially constructed realities."[4] Creswell lists several reasons to utilize a qualitative methodology.[5] First, the research questions for a qualitative study must begin with "what" and/or "how." Therefore, the research questions are as follows. What are the experiences of LGB and SSA students at Christian colleges and universities? How can Christian colleges and universities reduce marginalization of LGB and SSA students? Second, a qualitative study examines a fairly unexplored topic. The two research questions for this present study have not been explored prior to this research, and the topic of marginalization of LGB and SSA students at Christian colleges and universities is under-represented in research literature.[6] Third, a qualitative study emphasizes the role of the researcher as an active learner. The researcher for this present study sought to collect responses from participants in order to learn from the emerging data.[7]

To adequately address the complexity of the research questions, both qualitative and quantitative aspects were employed through a mixed

2. Newman et al., 168–69.

3. Creswell and Plano Clark, *Mixed Methods Research*, 60.

4. Newman et al., 170.

5. Creswell, *Qualitative Inquiry and Research Design*, 16–18.

6. Yarhouse et al., "Listening to Sexual Minorities," 99.

7. Creswell, 18.

methods approach.[8] Creswell and Plano Clark provided several reasons that justified the utilization of a mixed methods approach.[9] First, there was a need to enhance the primary method of a study with a secondary method. The primary method of this study was qualitative in nature, and the secondary method was quantitative in nature to enhance the study. Quantitative methodology is "a research paradigm designed to address questions that hypothesize relationships among variables that are measured frequently in numerical and objective ways."[10] Questions that are quantitative in nature can enhance the qualitative questions in understanding the experiences of LGB and SSA students at Christian colleges and universities. Second, there was a need to help explain the initial results. Some responses to open-ended questions produced two different distribution curves as opposed to one distribution curve, and answers to some quantitative questions assisted in analyzing those responses. The degree to which respondents held to a traditional view of sexuality (TVS) or a progressive view of sexuality (PVS), or the degree to which respondents agreed with the institutional policies on homosexuality, assisted in understanding some qualitative data.

The researcher chose a fixed mixed methods design over an emergent mixed methods design. Fixed mixed methods designs are "mixed methods studies where the use of quantitative and qualitative methods is determined and planned at the start of the research process, and the procedures are implemented as planned."[11] Emergent mixed methods designs are "found in mixed methods studies where the use of mixed methods arises due to issues that develop during the process of conducting the research."[12]

A mixed methods study "involves the collection or analysis of both quantitative and/or qualitative data in a single study in which the data are collected concurrently or sequentially, are given a priority, and involve the integration of the data at one or more stages in the process of research."[13] From this definition, Creswell and colleagues provide three variables that are a part of mixed methods research. First, mixed method data collection is either implemented concurrently or implemented sequentially. Second, the data in the research report (qualitative and quantitative) is either given

8. Newman et al., 168.

9. Creswell and Plano Clark, 7–11.

10. Newman et al., 170.

11. Creswell and Plano Clark, 54.

12. Ibid.

13. Creswell et al., "Advanced Mixed Methods Research Designs," 212.

equal priority or unequal priority (i.e., one is given priority or emphasis over the other). Third, integration of mixed methods occurs either during the data collection phase, during the data analysis phase, or during the data interpretation phase.

The researcher chose a concurrent transformative mixed method study design. This design's implementation of qualitative and quantitative data collection is concurrent. The research instrument was an online questionnaire that consisted of both open-ended and closed-ended questions. The priority placed on data is unequal with priority placed upon qualitative data. The open-ended questions provided answers to both research questions (experiences and recommendations). The closed-ended questions only enhanced the understanding of the data and provided the opportunity to compare the results between the different subgroups of participants. The integration of the two methods occurred in the interpretation stage. The qualitative data was first analyzed and then the quantitative data was incorporated in the interpretation stage as a way to compare data themes.

The researcher selected intramethod mixing over intermethod mixing. Intramethod mixing is "the concurrent or sequential use of a *single* method that includes both qualitative and quantitative components."[14] Intermethod mixing is "concurrently or sequentially mixing two or more methods."[15] Examples of intramethod mixing are the concurrent use of closed- and open-ended questions in a survey or the sequential use of a closed-ended questionnaire and an open-ended questionnaire. An example of intermethod mixing is a closed-ended questionnaire and interviews. Intramethod mixing is also known as "data triangulation" and intermethod mixing is also known as "method triangulation."[16]

Research Instrument and Data Collection Procedures

The research instrument was a mixed methods questionnaire (see Appendix A) focusing on the experiences of Christian college or university LGB and SSA students and on recommendations for Christian colleges and universities to become less marginalizing for LGB and SSA students. There are many options for mixed methods data collection, and a questionnaire is

---

14. Johnson and Turner, "Data Collection Strategies," 298.

15. Ibid.

16. Johnson and Turner, 298.

one of those options.[17] The researcher designed an online, self-report data collection instrument, which was filled out by participants. The questionnaire consisted of three sections: (1) demographic data; (2) LGB and SSA student experiences; and (3) recommendations.

The first section on demographic data contained eleven questions, which were mostly quantitative, such as, age, sex, race, student or alumnus/alumna, name of Christian college or university, year of graduation, residential status (i.e., did participant live in residence halls?), sexual identity, extent of being "out," and relationship status as a student. The relationship status question was modified from the Student Relationships Assessment developed by The Center for Relationship Enrichment for students at Christian colleges and universities.[18] Although the above questions were close-ended (multiple choice or drop-down menu), some questions (e.g., sex, race, sexual identity, and relationship status as a student) had an "Other" option and an area to fill in the blank. The first section on demographics contained only one open-ended question: "As a college or university student, why are or were you open or not open about your sexuality?"

The second section on LGB and SSA student experiences contained seven qualitative questions and nine quantitative questions. The first group of four questions was qualitative—"Describe any positive and/or negative experiences you've had as a sexual minority, college or university student"—delineated in four ways: (1) in the resident halls; (2) in the classroom; (3) as you interacted with your classmates; and (4) which were not covered above. The next two qualitative questions asked participants what chapel programming was available regarding singleness and sexuality and how it was helpful or not helpful. The next group of six questions covered institutional policies and were quantitative in nature. The first two questions simply asked the degree to which the participant agreed or disagreed with the lifestyle agreement and any additional institutional policy on homosexuality. The following four items asked participants to "Please indicate the degree to which you agree with the following statements" by selecting one of five options: agree, somewhat agree, somewhat disagree, disagree, or don't know. The four items were: (1) I believe God blesses monogamous unions between two people of the same sex; (2) I agree with my college or university's lifestyle agreement on homosexuality; (3) As a student, my college or university's lifestyle agreement on homosexuality makes or made

17. Johnson and Turner, 303.

18. The Center for Relationship Enrichment, "Student Relationships Assessment."

me feel marginalized and/or unsafe; and (4) I agree with my college or university's additional statement on sexuality which is in addition to the lifestyle agreement. These four items were followed by an open-ended question asking the participant to explain why there was agreement or disagreement with the university's statement(s) on homosexuality. The last three questions of this section on LGB and SSA student experiences was a three-item loneliness scale modified from the UCLA Loneliness Scale (questions 4, 10, and 16) of Dan Russell and colleagues' 1978 study among college students.[19] Marginalization is associated with social exclusion and the loneliness scale was a way to quantify a person feeling excluded or alone.

The third section on recommendations contained four qualitative questions. The first three questions asked participants what recommendations they would give to (1) faculty and administration, (2) residence life and student development staff, and (3) other college or university students "on how they can make your college or university a healthier environment for sexual minority students." The fourth question was: "What can your college or university do to communicate that it is a healthy and safe environment for sexual minority students before they even arrive on campus?"

The researcher struggled with what terminology to use for LGB and SSA students and alumni. The researcher was aware that the acronym "LGB" was not sufficiently inclusive. Several related studies revealed that not all SSA college and university students chose to identify as lesbian, gay, or bisexual.[20] In an attempt to be inclusive of those who do identify as LGB and those who do not identify as LGB but still experienced SSA, the term "sexual minority" was used.[21] However, the researcher acknowledged that "sexual minority" is a controversial term. This term seems to imply that racial minority and sexual minority are equivalent. Although there may be some congruence, there is also some incongruence. Since this debate goes beyond the scope of the project, the researcher decided not to use "sexual minority" as the primary way to refer to the participants. Rather, the acronyms LGB and SSA were utilized. Wentz and Wessel also utilized the two concepts of "students who feel same-sex attraction or who identify as

19. Russell et al., "Developing a Measure of Loneliness," 291–92.

20. Silverschanz et al., 182; Rankin et al., *2010 State,* 48; Yarhouse et al., "Sexual Identity," 3; Dean et al., 65, 73; Stratton et al., 9. For a more detailed discussion, see last section of Appendix E (literature review).

21. Silverschanz et al., 182; Yarhouse et al., "Listening to Sexual Minorities," 98; Dean et al., 65; Stratton et al., 9.

gay or lesbian."[22] The term sexual minority was only included in the report when it was found in related research literature or when quoted from the participants' responses.

Before proceeding with the study, the researcher obtained approval from the Institutional Review Board (IRB) of the university where he was pursuing his doctorate. The Bethel University IRB "seeks to ensure the respectful and ethical treatment of human participants in research."[23] Because the research topic was highly personal, involving issues of sexuality, the research was determined to be Level 1 (high). Level 1 requires review by the Bethel Institutional Review Board. Level 2 requires review only by the supervising department, and Level 3 simply requires review by the instructor or supervisor.[24] The researcher completed research ethics training through the Collaborative Institutional Training Initiative (CITI).[25] Along with the Human Subject Review Form and the research ethics training documentation of completion, the researcher also submitted the Informed Consent Form (see Appendix B) and the research instrument questions.

Because of the highly sensitive nature of the study, the researcher desired to minimize the risk of the participants' invasion of privacy by employing an online questionnaire using the Qualtrics platform.[26] Participation in this study and the information collected via the online questionnaire on Qualtrics was completely anonymous. Any information obtained in this study that could be identified with participants remained confidential. The names of the participants' Christian colleges and universities was not released or used in reports. The data collected from the questionnaires was stored in a Qualtrics-secure database. Participation in the research study was completely voluntary. Participants had the right to withdraw at any time or refuse to participate entirely without prejudice. Before being allowed to begin the online questionnaire, the participant needed to agree to the consent form. If the participant did not agree to the consent form, the participant was not allowed to continue. It was suggested that participants contact a licensed clinical professional counselor if they experienced emotional discomfort, distress, or negative emotions while participating in

22. Wentz and Wessel, 56.
23. Bethel University, "Institutional Review Board."
24. Bethel University, "Levels of Review."
25. Collaborative Institutional Training Initiative, "Home Page."
26. Qualtrics, "About Us."

this study. If participants were current students, they were encouraged to contact their school's counseling center if they experienced any distress.

The researcher sought to recruit a minimum of thirty LGB or SSA Christian college or university students and alumni to complete the online questionnaire. The recruitment strategy began through an existing, informal network of principal contacts at Christian colleges and universities where the researcher had spoken. These principal contacts were administrators, staff, faculty, alumni, or students and were given a letter (see Appendix C). The principal contact was asked to help recruit potential participants for the study by emailing a digital PDF letter to potential participants (see Appendix D). In this digital PDF letter for potential participants was a link to the consent form and questionnaire on the Qualtrics platform. The online questionnaire form assured the anonymity of the participants. Additional participants were gathered through a snowball sampling strategy. There were no inducements or rewards offered to participants before or after the study. The following two minimal purposive sampling criteria were established for the recruitment of potential participants. First, participants currently attend, or have attended within the past ten years, a Christian college or university that holds to a traditional view of sexuality (TVS) and has institutional policies prohibiting intimate sexual relations outside marriage between a husband and wife, including same-sex sexual practice. Second, participants are LGB or SSA. The goal was to recruit a minimum of thirty LGB or SSA Christian college or university students and alumni to complete the online questionnaire. Recruitment strategy consisted of purposive sampling.

Data Analysis Methodology

Although a mixed methods approach was taken, the researcher placed a priority upon the qualitative data. Therefore, the bulk of the data analysis focused upon the qualitative data. There are basically two approaches to qualitative data analysis.[27] A first approach focuses more on the language used by the participants by utilizing varieties of narrative and discourse analysis. A second approach focuses more on the content of what the participants have said and is "principally concerned with understanding their participants' lived experience from their own position."[28] Most qualitative

27. King and Horrocks, *Interviews in Qualitative Research*, 142.

28. King and Horrocks, 142.

or mixed methods studies fall into this second category (e.g., phenomeno-logical, grounded theory, or case studies). Nigel King and Christine Hor-rocks explain the principles of thematic analysis. Themes are "recurrent and distinctive features of participants' accounts, characterising particular perceptions and/or experiences, which the researcher sees as relevant to the research question."[29] It is important to balance within-case and cross-case analysis to avoid developing themes that are detached from the personal experiences of the participants or do not address the research question.

The researcher utilized the three stages of thematic analysis from King and Horrocks.[30] These three stages of thematic analysis did not necessarily progress in a sequential order. At times, there was a need to cycle back and forth between stages. Stage one of thematic data analysis was descriptive coding. The goal was to identify parts of the data that would help address the research question. The emphasis for this first stage was not to interpret but to describe what was of interest in the participants' accounts. The first step of this stage was to read through the answers at least once without attempting to code the data in order to become familiarized with the whole corpus of qualitative data. The second step was to highlight all the main points from the respondents' answers. The researcher utilized Dedoose, an online data analysis software for qualitative, quantitative, and mixed meth-ods research. Dedoose enabled the researcher to create highlighted por-tions or excerpts from the qualitative data. The excerpts were normally an entire sentence or several sentences. The third step was to define descrip-tive codes from the excerpts. These descriptive codes were key words that emerged directly from the excerpts. The goal was to use the respondents' words, avoiding speculation or interpretation of the data. The researcher exported the excerpts linked to the quantitative data into a spreadsheet and created the descriptive codes in the spreadsheet. The fourth step in stage one was to read through the data again to merge together any overlapping descriptive codes or define a new code. This process of defining, applying, and redefining descriptive codes was a cycle that continued from response to response throughout stage one of data analysis.

Stage two of thematic data analysis was interpretive coding. The goal was to define codes based on the interpretation of the data by grouping to-gether descriptive codes that shared some common meaning and creating an interpretive code that captured this common meaning. It was important

29. King and Horrocks, 150.
30. King and Horrocks, 152–58.

to refer back to the data behind the descriptive codes while creating the interpretive codes. The researcher was careful not to apply specific theoretical concepts or hypotheses into the coding at this stage. It was not uncommon for some descriptive codes to feed into more than one interpretive theme. The researcher created the interpretive codes in a spreadsheet from data exported out of Dedoose. The first step was to group similar descriptive codes together that shared a common meaning. The second step was to create a name for each group that should sufficiently summarize the meaning of the descriptive codes within that group. This new group name was an interpretive code. The third step was to apply the interpretive codes to the full data set. Similar to stage one, there was a cycle of adding, redefining, and reapplying interpretive codes from response to response throughout stage two of data analysis. This process was completed when the meaning offered in the data was thoroughly represented by the interpretive codes. Not all interpretive codes emerged from the research data. Some interpretive codes emerged from related and relevant research (see literature review in Appendix E).

Stage three of thematic data analysis was the development of overarching themes. The goal was to identify overarching themes that characterized key concepts from the data analysis process. These overarching themes emerged from the interpretive codes. At this point, the researcher began to apply theoretical concepts and hypotheses that were supported by the data. The first step was to develop key overarching themes for the data set as a whole from the interpretive codes and the project's theoretical stance. The researcher attempted to restrict the number of overarching themes between two to five. The second step was to construct tables to represent the relationships between the overarching themes, interpretive codes, and descriptive codes.

In review, the researcher employed a mixed methods study design with priority placed on the qualitative data. The research instrument was an online questionnaire consisting of three sections: (1) demographic data; (2) LGB and SSA student experiences; and (3) recommendations. The recruitment strategy consisted of purposive sampling. The data analysis methodology was based upon King and Horrocks' three stages of thematic analysis: (1) descriptive coding; (2) interpretive coding; and (3) overarching themes.

—— 4 ——

Presentation and Synthesis of Data

I N THIS CHAPTER, THE researcher analyzed and evaluated the data from the online questionnaire. In addition, major themes were identified from the experiences and recommendations from LGB and SSA Christian college and university student and alumni participants.. The first section was an analysis of the quantitative data, which provided a description of the respondents. The second section was an analysis of the qualitative data. Three overarching themes emerged: (1) disclosure of sexuality; (2) experiences; and (3) recommendations.

Quantitative Data: Description of the Respondents

Between April and December 2013, 104 people accessed the online questionnaire. Five people did not provide consent, and 17 people, although providing consent, did not answer any questions. Two respondents were not included because they had graduated more than 10 years ago. Therefore, the total sample size was 80 ($N = 80$). Those who completed the questionnaire were 65 percent of the total sample ($n = 52$), and 35 percent partially completed the questionnaire ($n = 28$). In statistics, N is the number of units in the population or total sample size, while n is the number of units in a sample or subgroup. N was also used to refer to all respondents who answered a particular question. Although data from partially completed questionnaires could have been omitted, the emphasis of this study was upon the qualitative data and the researcher decided to include all data from questionnaires (partial or complete) that included qualitative data.

While all participants were young adults, almost two-thirds were between 18–22 years old (see figure 4.1). Males were overrepresented with almost 3 to every 1 female (see figure 4.2). One respondent answered "Other: transgender female." The majority of respondents were Caucasian (see figure 4.3). Multi-ethnicities represented were Caucasian and Asian ($n = 2$), Caucasian and African ($n = 1$), Caucasian and Hispanic ($n = 1$), Caucasian and Pacific Islander ($n = 1$), and Hispanic and Asian ($n = 1$). Participants were from 32 different Christian colleges and universities. All institutions held to a traditional view of sexuality (TVS) and had policies prohibiting extramarital sexual relations. The colleges and universities were spread across 15 states with over half of the respondents attending Midwest institutions (see figures 4.4 and 4.5). Approximately two-thirds (61.3 percent, $n = 49$) of the respondents were current students, while 33.8 percent were alumni ($n = 27$) and four attended for at least one full year but never graduated (see table 4.1).

Figure 4.1 Age Distribution of Respondents (n = 77)

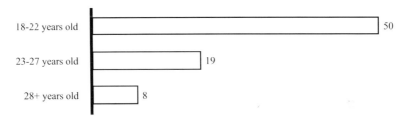

Figure 4.2 Sex Distribution of Respondents (n = 78)

Figure 4.3 Race Distribution of Respondents (n = 80)

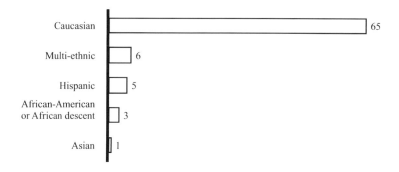

Figure 4.4 State Distribution of Schools and Respondents (n = 15)

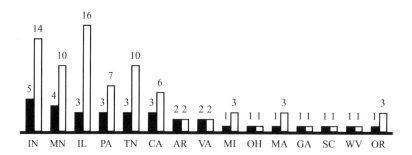

Figure 4.5 Regional Distribution of Schools and Respondents

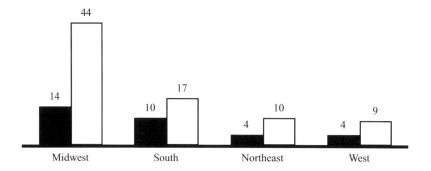

Table 4.1 Graduating Class Distribution of Current Students and Alumni

Current Students (n = 49)								
2017	2016	2015	2014	2013				
4	11	13	12	9				
Alumni (n = 27)								
2013	2012	2011	2010	2009	2008	2007	2006	2004
9	5	1	2	3	1	3	1	2

While on campus, most respondents had lived in the residence halls (92.5 percent, $n = 74$), with only 6 replying that they had not. For the majority of the time as a college or university student, 66.3 percent of the respondents were single and not dating ($n = 53$), 16.3 percent were casually dating ($n = 13$), 12.5 percent were seriously dating ($n = 10$), 1 was "in a serious committed relationship," 1 was "secretly dating," 1 "fluctuated between all of these options," and 1 did not provide an answer. Around one-third of the respondents identified as gay or lesbian (36.3 percent) and another third responded having same sex attractions (32.5 percent). The remaining were bisexual, gay and celibate, and "Other" (see figure 4.6). Fifty-eight respondents only told a few about their sexuality (72.5 percent), while 14 were fairly open (17.5 percent) and 8 told nobody (ten percent).

Figure 4.6 Sexuality Distribution of Respondents (n = 80)

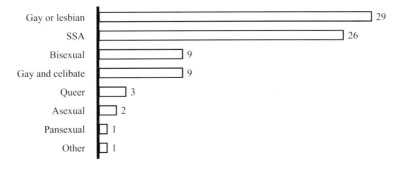

Of those who replied ($n = 64$), 58 were aware of the lifestyle agreement (90.6 percent) and 6 were not (9.4 percent). Twenty-two knew about their school's additional statement on homosexuality, 20 knew there was no statement, and 22 did not know if their school had an additional statement. There was a fairly even split between those who agreed that God blesses same-sex unions, holding to a progressive view of sexuality (PVS), and those who disagreed that God blesses same-sex unions, holding to a TVS. The percentage of participants who held to a PVS was 37.5 ($n = 24$), and the percentage of participants who held to a TVS was 40.6 ($n = 26$). However, slightly more respondents disagreed with their school's lifestyle agreement on homosexuality (42.2 percent, $n = 27$) and agreed or somewhat agreed that it made them feel marginalized and/or unsafe (66.7 percent, $n = 42$). Among those who replied, most disagreed or did not know whether they agreed or disagreed with their school's additional statement on sexuality (see table 4.2). Among respondents who indicated a level of agreement for the items about whether God blesses same-sex unions and whether they agree with the school's lifestyle statement, a negative correlation was observed ($n = 56$, Spearman correlation coefficient = -0.89). Those who believe that God blesses same-sex unions tended to disagree with the lifestyle statement and those who believe homosexuality is a sin tended to agree with the lifestyle statement.

Table 4.2 Responses to Questions C9 - C12

	Agree	Some-what agree	Some-what disagree	Disagree	Don't know
C9. I believe God blesses monogamous unions between two people of the same sex (i.e., it is NOT a sin). ($n = 64$)	24	7	3	26	4
C10. I agree with my college or university's lifestyle agreement on homosexuality. ($n = 64$)	18	9	5	27	5
C11. As a student, my college or university's lifestyle agreement on homosexuality makes or made me feel marginalized and/or unsafe. ($n = 63$)	24	18	5	15	1

C12. I agree with my college or university's additional statement on sexuality which is in addition to the lifestyle agreement. (If your school doesn't have one, leave this blank). (n = 31)	5	3	3	10	10

In scoring the loneliness scale (questions C14 to C16), "Hardly ever" was given the value of 1, "Sometimes" 2, and "Often" 3. Respondents' three values were totaled and analyzed. The average total value was 7.0, but the most frequently occurring total value or mode was 9 (27 percent, n = 17). The majority of the respondents scored high on the loneliness scale. See table 4.3 and figure 4.7.

Table 4.3 Loneliness Scale: Questions C14 - C16 (n = 63)

	Mean/Standard Deviation	Median	Mode	Range
C14. How often do or did you feel that you lacked companionship as a sexual minority, college or university student?	2.4 ± 0.6	2	3	1-3
C15. How often do or did you feel left out as a sexual minority, college or university student?	2.2 ± 0.8	2	3	1-3
C16. How often do or did you feel isolated from others as a sexual minority, college or university student?	2.4 ± 0.6	2	3	1-3
Total Values from Questions C14–C16	7.0 ± 1.7	7	9	3-9

Figure 4.7 Loneliness Scale: Distribution of Total Values and Respondents (n = 63)

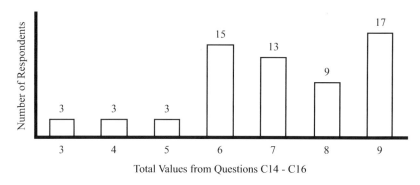

There were three major findings that emerged from the quantitative data. First, there was diversity among respondents in the way they identified their own sexuality, in their views related to the morality of same-sex relationships, and in their agreement with institutional policies on same-sex sexual practice. Second, a negative correlation was observed among respondents who indicated a level of agreement for the items about whether God blesses same-sex unions and whether they agree with the school's lifestyle statement. Those who believe that God blesses same-sex unions tended to disagree with the lifestyle statement and those who believe same-sex sexual practice is sinful tended to agree with the lifestyle statement. Third, the majority of the respondents reported high scores on the loneliness scale.

Qualitative Data: Disclosure of Sexuality, Experiences, and Recommendations

The qualitative data was coded following King and Horrocks' three stages of thematic analysis: (1) descriptive coding; (2) interpretive coding; and (3) overarching themes.[1] To determine the descriptive codes, the researcher first read through the answers once without attempting to code the data in order to become familiar with the whole corpus of qualitative data. An online data analysis software was utilized to excerpt main points from respondents. Key words were pulled directly from the excerpts to create the descriptive codes. To develop the interpretive codes, the researcher grouped similar descriptive codes together and created an interpretive code. Lastly,

1. King and Horrocks, 152–58.

the researcher applied theoretical concepts and hypotheses and developed three overarching themes: (1) disclosure of sexuality; (2) experiences; and (3) recommendations. These overarching themes emerged from nine sub-themes and twenty-seven interpretive codes (see table 4.4). Each of these three overarching themes was discussed below with excerpts from participants' own words. The researcher copied verbatim from the participants' responses except identifiable data (e.g., college or university names) was removed and spelling or grammatical errors were corrected. Square brackets were used when removing identifiable data or correcting spelling, grammar, or style issues (e.g., changing numerals to text).

Table 4.4 Overarching Themes, Sub-themes, and Interpretive Codes

Overarching theme	Sub-theme	Interpretive Code
Disclosure of sexuality	Reasons to hide	Fear others' response Negative climate Lack of readiness Fear disciplinary action
	Reasons to be open	Trustworthy and supportive friends Comfortable with sexuality Helping others Helping oneself
Experiences	Classmates	Hurtful comments Supportive friends Nudity or joking around
	Employees	Professors Staff
	Chapels and student programming	Sexuality Singleness
Recommendations	Institutional policies	Disagree Agree
	Campus climate	Awareness and attitudes Hurtful comments Nudity and immodesty Singleness

Recommenda-tions	Programming	Inform and train Consider other interpretations Singleness
	Groups and mentoring	Support groups Advocacy groups Mentoring

Overarching Theme: Disclosure of Sexuality

The first overarching theme emerged from two sub-themes, eight interpretive codes and sixty-eight descriptive codes. Seventy-eight respondents provided answers that fell into this overarching theme ($N = 78$). The two sub-themes were: (1) reasons to hide; and (2) reasons to be open. There was a common sentiment that it would have been better to be more open about their sexuality if they had been able. One SSA male student wrote, "My prayer is that I find the strength to open up to any of my fellow brothers so that they can help me overcome such." Another SSA male alumnus explained, "I only wish I had chosen to open up sooner. Walking through those first few years of this journey would have been so much healthier in the context of Christian community."

Sub-theme: Reasons to Hide

The first sub-theme consisted of four interpretive codes and forty-two descriptive codes (see table 4.5). The four interpretive codes were: (1) fear others' response; (2) negative climate; (3) lack of readiness; and (4) fear disciplinary action. By far, the most responses fell under the first interpretive code, fear others' response. The majority of respondents allowed a select few to know about their sexuality (72.5 percent, $n = 58$, $N = 80$), and eight respondents did not let anybody know (10 percent). There were more reasons for wanting to hide than wanting to be open.

Table 4.5 Sub-theme: Reasons to Hide

Sub-theme	Interpretive Code	Descriptive Code
Reasons to hide	Fear others' response	Fear of . . . being branded an outcast being cut off being demeaned being harassed being judged being made fun of being ostracized being preached at being rejected being treated differently it going over poorly losing friends persecution poor reception relationship changing
	Negative climate	Condemned to hell Derogatory words and jokes Did not trust others Harassment Homophobic Hostile Inherently wrong No other options Not open Not safe Taboo Worst sin
	Lack of readiness	Afraid to identify with the attraction Coming to terms with it Didn't want to deal with it Not comfortable Not yet come out Only recently came out Still figuring it all out Still reconciling Wanted to ignore it

Reason to Hide	Fear disciplinary action	Fear of . . . being expelled being kicked out being required to go to counseling being required to live alone being thrown out needing administration attention

Interpretive code: Fear others' response. Thirty-seven respondents chose to hide their sexuality because they feared how others would respond (47.4 percent, $N = 78$). This was the most widely shared comment within this sub-theme of reasons to hide. The majority of respondents who were not open about their sexuality expressed this in one way or another. Several did not want to be judged for being LGB or SSA. One male, gay and celibate alumnus wrote, "I was terrified that I would be judged and ostracized for something that I didn't want and something that wasn't in my control." A gay male alumnus said, "I was convinced that I'd be judged and excluded if I were to be open about my sexuality." A bisexual female alumna expressed her fear this way: "To share with anyone else I didn't feel would go over well and that I would be [judged] or shunned."

Respondents also feared rejection from other classmates. "I didn't feel like I would be understood or heard if I were to come out as struggling with same-sex attraction. I thought that I would at the very least be rejected by peers and maybe even made fun of," wrote a gay male alumnus. A gay and celibate male student said, "It is very easy for me to imagine being branded as an outcast for coming out." Respondents also were afraid of being demeaned and harassed. One gay male student wrote, "Being anything but straight is seen as a negative characteristic and as soon as people learn that about you they demean you a little bit more." Another male SSA student concurred, "There are a great deal of Evangelicals here that would [harass] me if they knew that I was queer."

Although many of the answers were perceived fears and not from actual harassment, one lesbian alumna did experience a negative response. "I didn't come out to many more people after my initial openness because of the poor reception I received from those to whom I was closest." Several respondents expected that their relationships would change if they opened up about their sexuality. A lesbian student explained, "I was worried about how my relationships with my teammates, family, and friends would change." "I was worried that some of them would either cut off contact with me completely or would treat me differently," wrote a bisexual female alumna. One gay male student said, "Being treated different or worse is not a risk we want to take in telling those around us. It is like a gamble, tell a friend and see how differently they treat you." A female SSA student explained, "I also am in the ministry department and although a professor and the chair of the department know, it could very well go over poorly if students found out." Even students who agreed with the policies against same-sex sexual practice were afraid to be open for fear of others' response. A male SSA student who did not tell anybody about his sexuality wanted help with his struggles from his peers but wrote, "I will face persecution and the feeling of shame and guilt from my fellow peers, rather than helping me overcome this struggle." A male SSA student was honest with a select few friends but was afraid of being attacked from opposite sides by those who would either "preach at me or ask me to join a pride group." For a gay male student, losing his closest friends would have been unbearable.

> The biggest fear in coming out to close friends is that they will shy away from treating you as they did previously or walk on eggshells around you, or perhaps avoid you completely. I was terrified to tell close friends for this reason; I couldn't bear to lose some of the most meaningful friendships in my life.

The most common reason given by respondents for feeling a need to hide their sexuality was a fear of others' response. This included fear of being judged, fear of being rejected, and fear that relationships would change.

Interpretive code: Negative climate. Twenty-one respondents chose to hide their sexuality because of the negative climate at their Christian college or university campus (26.9 percent, $N = 78$). Nine stated that the environment was hostile and not safe. A female SSA student who allowed a select few to know about her sexuality spoke up about several of her friends who were not open, and some even were considering suicide.

> They do not feel they can talk about their experiences with anyone in a leadership role because they know that this isn't a safe and open community for them, and they're right—officially it's not. So, now we have students contemplating suicide because they think if they were to die they would stop having these feelings—that is not a hyperbole by the way, but real thoughts of real students. Or they significantly limit their interactions with the [school] community and become isolated.

A lesbian alumna wrote, "I wasn't open because I didn't feel safe on campus with most of the professors . . . or with most of the conservative students." A male SSA student who told nobody about his sexuality as a student explained, "The Christian college environment especially living in the dorms is hostile and homophobic to the issues of homosexuality." Silverschanz and colleagues made a distinction between "personal" and "ambient" harassment. Personal harassment was directed at an individual, not necessarily the respondent. Ambient harassment was not directed at an individual, yet heard by the respondent.[2] A gay male alumnus who came out his senior year explained that he experienced more than just ambient harassment.

> For the first [three] years, I was not comfortable with my orientation, and I feared what [certain] members of the student body would say about me. I also experienced sexual [harassment] due to my orientation during my freshmen year, so that also instilled a sense of fear.

It seemed from the responses that most of the harassment was not directed at an individual, but that most of the harassment was indirect or ambient. Derogatory words and gay jokes created a negative and unsafe climate for participants. A gay male alumnus wrote, "Even though I didn't call myself 'gay' at that point, the derogatory use of the word made me feel unsafe." A gay and celibate male student said, "I would not be open because of crude jokes and derogatory uses of the word 'gay' and it made me feel uncomfortable and angry." A gay male student realized that being more open may have helped his classmates stop the derogatory remarks, but the slurs only made things worse.

> Heteronormativity and LGBT slurs are shockingly rampant at my institution, particular in the male side of the residence halls. This unwelcoming atmosphere [most] likely would have been more subdued if my [floor mates] were aware of my sexuality, but as such, it silenced me further because I did not feel safe or welcomed on my freshman and sophomore floors.

For this respondent, the derogatory slurs made him hide his sexuality and hiding his sexuality only perpetuated the derogatory slurs. It was a vicious cycle.

Respondents expressed that their classmates viewed same-sex sexual practice to be the worst sin and anything related to homosexuality was

2. Silverschanz et al., 180.

disgusting and inherently wrong. This compounded their fear of being open. A female SSA student wrote, "I know it is a sin and going to a Christian college people look down upon you, like your sin is worse than theirs." "[My classmates] thought anything related to homosexuality was disgusting and wrong," explained a female SSA student. A gay male alumnus said, "I was specifically silent because of the way in which many people associated a non-majority sexuality as inherently wrong even though I was not necessarily acting on my feelings." A gay and celibate male student felt attacked by the more conservative students but also did not receive support from the more liberal students.

> I think what's so hard about coming out at a Christian college is knowing that you will deal with a lot of different crap from a lot of different people. One side will say "Sorry dude, but you're kinda condemned to hell" (show me where that is in the Bible) and another side will say "It's how you were made and check out all these churches that will back you up!"

A female SSA student said that her closeted friends "felt as though they had no other options. The topic of sexuality, and homosexuality specifically, is so taboo on campus that there are few to no resources or other places to talk about these subjects and questions."

Respondents felt that they could not trust others as well. A queer male alumnus who did not let anybody know about his sexuality explained, "I don't think I trusted anyone enough to really sit down and have that whole conversation." A female SSA student wrote,

> In weekly meetings with the other RAs [resident assistants], we would share our personal stories as well as any conflicts we were dealing with. Every single week I would hear RAs complain about various personal matters but never felt like I could open up about myself. I didn't trust them to not tell anyone else and I couldn't see them being at all understanding or sympathetic.

Participants explained that their campus was not safe, other students used derogatory words, homosexuality is viewed as the worst sin, and they could not trust others. This created a negative climate in which participants felt a need to hide their sexuality.

Interpretive code: Lack of readiness. Eighteen respondents chose to hide their sexuality because they were not yet ready to disclose their sexuality for various reasons (23.1 percent, $N = 78$). Several did not disclose their sexuality because they were not comfortable with their sexuality. A gay and celibate male alumnus who had not told anybody about his sexuality explained, "Part of this was me, [because] I didn't have the courage to talk to anyone. Part of it was I never felt comfortable to tell anyone about it." A male SSA student wrote, "I do not feel comfortable yet with that being 'common knowledge' among my family and friends." One gay male alumnus said, "I was not comfortable with my orientation." Several participants did not even want to acknowledge that they had gay feelings. A gay and celibate male alumnus explained,

> I also just didn't want to discuss it because bringing it up would mean that I would have to deal with it and acknowledge it. For a long time, I tried to separate my sexuality from the rest of my life and if I talked about it with someone else, that would make it something real, something that didn't just concern me anymore. I didn't want to deal with my sexuality at all, so I didn't talk about it for a long time.

Others wanted to ignore it and were afraid to identify with the attractions. A gay and celibate male alumnus said, "I was able to ignore it by not talking about it." A female SSA student who was not open with anybody reasoned, "I am afraid to identify and/or come to terms with the attraction."

Some respondents lacked readiness to be open because they had not yet come out to themselves or their family. A bisexual male student stated, "I have not yet come out to my family members due to their religious beliefs and being open on campus would certainly get back to them before I am ready." One gay male student wrote, "I just recently identified myself as gay," and another agreed, "I also have only recently come out to myself." The process of coming to terms with one's sexuality takes time and during that time, respondents would not feel a need to share about it. A gay male student wrote, "It took me a while to come to terms with my own sexuality, and when I identified as SSA, I didn't share about it much." One gay and celibate male alumnus explained, "I was still engaged in reconciling myself to my sexuality." A male SSA student wrote, "I am still working through everything. I am not going to make a sweeping declaration about myself if I am still figuring it all out." "I also had not yet come to terms with it yet," explained another gay male alumnus.

There were four main reasons that respondents gave to explain why they were not yet ready to be open. First, they were not comfortable with their sexuality. Second, they wanted to ignore it all. Third, they had not yet or had just come out. Fourth, they were still figuring it all out.

Interpretive code: Fear disciplinary action. Nine respondents chose to hide their sexuality because they were afraid of being punished or disciplined by the school (11.5 percent, $N = 78$). A male SSA student wrote, "There have been people kicked out of my university for engaging in homosexual behavior, and it scares the hell out of me, so I have to stay in hiding until I graduate." A lesbian alumna explained, "I was afraid they would throw me out if they knew I was even tempted in that way, let alone that I had a steady girlfriend." Other respondents also feared being expelled for simply experiencing same-sex attractions. One male SSA student who told no one at his school about his sexuality said,

> I was not open because I felt shame and unclean. I am [a] follower
> of Christ and Christ followers should not have those feelings. Also,
> I was afraid of what people would think and do if they found out.
> Would I be [kicked] out of school or the ministry department?

A gay male alumnus recalled, "I was also afraid that if a resident assistant found out, I would have to talk to some administrator. I sincerely thought I could be kicked out simply for admitting my attractions."

The fear of punishment was not just being kicked out of school, but respondents were also afraid that they would be required to go to counseling. A female SSA student wrote, "The school doesn't have a good reputation in how it deals with questions of sexuality (either requiring counseling or asking students to leave)." A bisexual female alumna explained, "I think it is a bit harsh to make students, who identify themselves as homosexual or bisexual, to have counseling if they wish to attend this college." Not only was a gay male alumnus afraid of being punished, but he had heard that gays and lesbians were not allowed to live with others. "There were rumors of gay students being expelled and/or being required to attend counseling. Additionally, gay students were required to live in their own dorm room [alone]."

Fear of disciplinary action consisted of participants afraid of being kicked out or expelled, forced into counseling, or being placed into a solo room.

Sub-theme: Reasons to Be Open

The second sub-theme for reasons to be open, consisted of four interpretive codes and twenty-six descriptive codes (see table 4.6). The four interpretive codes were: (1) trustworthy and supportive friends; (2) comfortable with sexuality; (3) helping others; and (4) helping oneself. The interpretive codes are explained in order of prevalence, beginning with the first interpretive code with the most responses. Only fourteen respondents were fairly open about their sexuality (17.5 percent). More respondents allowed a select few to know about their sexuality and they also provided reasons for being open about their sexuality with others.

Table 4.6 Sub-theme: Reasons to Be Open

Sub-theme	Interpretive Code	Descriptive Code
Reasons to be open	Trustworthy and supportive friends	Compassionate Developed relationship Know me Loving Not judged Safe Supportive Trust
	Comfortable with sexuality	Be honest Being myself Did not want to lie Important part of me Integrate my sexuality More comfortable
	Helping others	Change perceptions Face the reality Help people understand
		Gift to be shared Help others who struggle Mentoring others with same sex attractions

Reasons to be open	Helping oneself	Emotional health
		Found catharsis
		Not healthy to keep everything inside
		Ask for prayer
		Needed help
		Needed to talk things out

Interpretive code: Trustworthy and supportive friends. Nineteen respondents chose to be open about their sexuality because of friends who were trustworthy, supportive, and safe (24.4 percent, $N = 78$). A male SSA student stated, "There were a few I shared with, but only if I felt safe." A lesbian alumna wrote, "I told a select few of my friends that I knew I could trust." One gay and celibate male student recalled,

> It [depended] on how safe I felt talking to others about my sexuality. When I felt like someone was caring and willing to support me in my struggle, I talked to them. It helped to know a person before I talked with them because they knew me as me and not "gay."

"I felt that if people did not know this important part of me, then they were not really people I could count on or trust," a lesbian student explained. Respondents would open up to their friends if they would not feel judged. A queer male student said, "I have only come out to those I know would be supportive or at least would listen carefully and suspend their ability to judge." A male SSA student concurred: "I am open with people I feel are safe to talk to, who won't judge me for something I don't understand and have little control of. I am open when I feel like a person might support me."

Having a developed friendship was an important aspect respondents gave for additional reasons to be open. An SSA student explained, "I would be open about sharing my past with people I had developed more of a relationship with." A bisexual alumnus believed that being open enriched the friendship bond. "I did come to feel that my relationships were deeper when I disclosed my sexuality." Similarly, a gay male alumnus stated, "I found that I could not be honest with my friends or feel like we had a genuine relationship without telling them about my sexuality." Although respondents were fearful of how others would respond if they disclosed their sexuality, several respondents expressed that those to whom they opened up were loving and compassionate. A bisexual female student wrote, "[There were] so many positive reactions from my classmates. [They] [loved] me and [listened] to my story." A male SSA student expressed, "So far, everyone I've confided in has been encouraging and compassionate."

Interpretive code: Comfortable with sexuality. Fifteen respondents chose to be open about their sexuality because they felt comfortable about their sexuality (19.2 percent, $N = 78$). A male SSA student wrote, "I think the more I am open, the more comfortable I will be with it, and hopefully the more encouraged others will be." A lesbian student believed that her sexuality was an "important part of me." "However, as I began to open up to others, with relatively few negative consequences, I felt more confident in my identity," another lesbian student said. A gay male alumnus wrote,

> I chose to become more open about my sexuality because I knew it was a defining part of who I am as a person. While it is not the defining part of who I am, it certainly has played a major role in my development as a person. I felt like if I wanted to live as a fully honest individual that I needed to share this part of my journey as well.

Honesty was a key aspect for respondents as they opened up about their sexuality. A gay and celibate male student expressed, "I wanted to be honest and open with those closest to me, especially those who I walk closely in community with." A gay male student stated, "I don't want [to] lie anymore," and another gay male student agreed, "being myself is important." A gay male student wrote, "I was tired of trying to hide who I was, and felt like I was living a lie. Once I stopped hiding, I felt like I could breathe and finally be who I was comfortably." Integration was important for one gay and celibate male alumnus: "It's been beneficial because it's allowed me to really integrate my sexuality into the rest of my life in a meaningful way."

Interpretive code: Helping others. Sixteen respondents chose to be open about their sexuality because they wanted to help others (20.5 percent, $N = 78$). This interpretive code was split into two groups. The first group focused more on advocacy and wanted to help others change their perceptions regarding LGB people. A queer male alumnus wrote, "I wanted to be open to start dialogues about the church and minority sexualities, a relationship I thought was in need of a lot of reconciliation. I was open because I was hoping to make a change in people's perception of LGBTQ students." A pansexual transgender female student said,

> I have a duty to pave the way for future students. I wish to change the hearts and minds of students, faculty and administration. I also consider it essential that my identities do not stay in the realm of ideas, but I want every person to connect a face to these identities.

"I believe it is time for Christian students to understand more fully the issue of sexuality," explained a male SSA student. One gay male alumnus stated, "I also feel like I have been given a certain life experience that not many people know much about, especially in a Christian subculture. Thus if I could help people understand better, I could help build bridges." A female student explained, "I love being who I am around the people on this campus and honestly enjoy forcing them to face the reality of having an openly gay student on campus."

The second group focused more on support and wanted to help others who struggle with same-sex attractions. A male SSA student wrote,

> Being able to share my struggle with others, especially those who share that struggle, has been greatly encouraging. . . . I do want to become more open about it, because I think that would increase my availability to help others who also struggle.

A bisexual male student explained that when he disclosed his sexuality, "each time has been for a specific ministry opportunity of some kind. Whether it [was a] family member, helping a friend to understand the subject better, confiding in a friend, or mentoring others with [same-sex attractions]." A bisexual male student explained, "I was open about my struggles with bisexuality to some people due to my conviction that my testimony could help others." A male SSA student said, "I have been taking steps to be more open to select people so that my story can benefit others." "I was open about my sexuality with those who asked. I believe that my story is a gift to be shared and in the words of Paul, I want to 'testify to the gospel of God's grace,'" explained a male SSA alumnus. Although the first group focused more on advocacy and the second group on support, both groups had a desire to help others.

Interpretive code: Helping oneself. Fourteen respondents chose to be open about their sexuality because they wanted to help themselves (17.9 percent, $N = 78$). Similar to the preceding interpretive code, this code was divided into two groups. The first group expressed that keeping their sexuality hidden would be detrimental to their mental, emotional, and/or spiritual health. A gay male student wrote, "I am open with only close

friends because it is not mentally healthy for me to keep everything inside."
A bisexual female student stated, "There comes a point where continuing
to hide my sexuality became unhealthy both emotionally and spiritually."
A gay and celibate male student confided that he struggled with depression
when he was not able to be open. "I'm open about it because hiding my
sexuality contributes heavily to depressive spells."

The second group expressed that they disclosed their sexuality because they desired help from others. A female SSA student wrote, "I told
a few close people because I was overwhelmed and needed help handling
the whole thing." One gay male student explained, "I need to talk things
out and hear advice from close friends I trust." Another gay and celibate
male student stated, "There's no way that I can voice my struggles or ask
for prayer in a way I'm satisfied with without my friends knowing about
my sexuality."

Summary: Disclosure of Sexuality (Overarching Theme)

There were three major findings that emerged from the overarching theme
of disclosure of sexuality. First, the majority of the respondents were not
completely open about their sexuality (either not open with anybody or
open with a select few). In addition, there were more reasons given to hide
their sexuality than to be open about their sexuality. Second, respondents
hid their sexuality because (1) they were afraid how others would respond,
(2) the campus climate was so negative, (3) they were not ready, or (4) they
were afraid of being disciplined by the school or being forced into counseling. Third, respondents were open about their sexuality because (1) they
had trustworthy and supportive friends, (2) they were comfortable with
their sexuality, (3) they wanted to help others, or (4) they wanted to help
themselves.

Overarching Theme: Experiences

The second overarching theme emerged from three sub-themes, seven
interpretive codes, and forty descriptive codes. Fifty-three respondents
provided answers that fell into this overarching theme ($N = 53$). The three
sub-themes were (1) classmates, (2) employees, and (3) chapels and student
programming.

Sub-theme: Classmates

The first sub-theme consisted of three interpretive codes and twenty descriptive codes (see table 4.7). The three interpretive codes were (1) hurtful comments, (2) supportive friends; and (3) nudity or joking around. The interpretive codes are explained in order of prevalence beginning with the first interpretive code with the most responses.

Table 4.7 Sub-theme: Classmates

Sub-theme	Interpretive Code	Descriptive Code
Classmates	Hurtful comments	Fag Gay jokes Going to hell Homophobic It's a choice Sin Slurs That's so gay
	Supportive friends	Accepting Encouraging Loving Supportive Understanding Welcoming
	Nudity or joking around	Community bathrooms/showers Flash genitals Homoeroticism Joking around Naked Nudity

Interpretive code: Hurtful comments. Three-quarters of the respondents reported hurtful comments from fellow students (75.5 percent, $n = 40$, $N = 53$). The majority of the hurtful comments were ambient (not directed toward the hearer), but there were a few personal hurtful comments directed at respondents. A gay and celibate male alumnus told this story:

> I led singing in chapel sometimes, and one time a fellow student and I were in an elevator going up to the dorm area. It was just the two of us. We didn't know each other well, but he looked at me and

asked, "Are you gay?" "No," I replied sheepishly. He asked this over and over. I was trapped in the elevator with him and extremely intimidated. I kept denying anything. "Well, are you bi?" he finally asked. "No," I replied. He then expressed disgust about how the school was letting gay people lead singing in chapel as he exited the elevator.

Another gay male student wrote about his experience.

I ran for freshman class president my first year. A student walked past my poster and made a comment to his friends, "I can't believe this fag is running." It was the first time I felt completely marginalized on my campus, went to an empty room and cried.

A gay male student explained, "People would always make little digs at me for being gay." A lesbian student stated, "I have also had people tell me that I am going to hell for being gay."

Although the majority of the hurtful comments were not personal, the ambient remarks were numerous. A queer male alumnus recalled, "Comments, homophobic actions and remarks that were not even aimed at me, but were a normal part of life. Lots of tiny moments that were despairing." A bisexual male commented,

I have heard several negative remarks toward sexual minority students (not students in particular, as there are no open sexual minority students at my school, but rather those who struggle with non-heterosexual attractions in general) in my biblical hermeneutics class, and some scoffing whenever it was brought up in my intro to sociology class.

A gay male student communicated, "I hate it when people say 'That's so gay' or 'faggot.' These things should not be said." A lesbian alumna described the tone and metaphor students often use when talking about LGB and SSA issues.

They like to talk about the "culture war" and conflate it with spiritual warfare. Christians, especially of college age, are soldiers in this war to win back the culture and the country for Christ. Unfortunately, the undertone of these slogans must be that Christians are the good guys, and anyone who disagrees with what we believe in any way must be the enemy. You cannot negotiate with the enemy, and seeming to fraternize with the enemy is a grave sin.

She also recalled a time in class where she was "reduced to tears."

> We were discussing *Pride and Prejudice* and whether it would have been right for Mr. Bennet to throw Lydia out after her tryst. I introduced the idea that perhaps a better modern-day equivalent would be whether it is right to throw your son out if you discover he is gay. Oh boy, it got heated really fast. The most numerous and loudest voices were all for casting out the son "for his own good." And their arguments for why it was for his own good were . . . awful. And yes, I cried. Because sometimes there is no reasoning with people nor appealing to their hearts, and that was such a day. I pray for the children of the people in that classroom.

Other students would make comments that homosexuality was a choice. A gay male alumnus said,

> We wound up talking more generally about homosexuality, and one of my classmates said that she just couldn't believe that being gay wasn't a choice. It took a lot of self-control to not bite her head off. I wanted to yell at her, "Do you think I chose this? Do you think I want this? Why would I possibly want this?!" I wanted so badly to be able to say something to that effect, but I didn't want to reveal my deeply personal connection to the topic of sexual identity.

A gay male student reflected, "Many of my floor mates had plenty to say on the fact of homosexuality. That it is a 'life choice,' that it's a lifestyle that homosexuals choose for themselves. But who chooses any of that?"

There were also some hurtful comments that were spiritual in nature. A female SSA alumna reflected, "From most of the discussions I heard, the majority opinion was that people with homosexual tendencies/preferences were going straight to hell." One gay male student wrote,

> Most people on campus seem to feel that I should be internally tormented by my sexuality, and should either be struggling to overcome it or should decide to live a celibate life. So when I tell them that neither is true for me, that's when I get arguments thrown at me and Bible verses quoted at me. It can be hard being a non-celibate gay student on a Christian campus.

Some students had good intentions, but their comments hurt and were not helpful. A gay male student revealed,

> Sometimes people will ask me how I'm doing spiritually—like if I've been praying or reading my bible. Their concern comes from a good place, but I can tell they think I'm in a constant state of

turmoil over my sexuality, and that I'm angry at God about everything. Granted, I am not happy with God, but I would rather people meet me where I am instead of thinking they need to heal me or something. Sometimes being a good friend is letting someone get better on their own time.

A male SSA alumnus stated something very similar.

> It comes in friends saying they want to learn how to love gay people but never once considering that maybe what gay people want is not to have every conversation about homosexuality end in a restatement of their [traditional] conclusion that it's wrong and instead just want someone to care enough to listen to what their story is, to how they've experienced marginalization because of their sexual identity.

An SSA female remarked, "Most of the students at school like to use the phrase, "Hate the sin, love the sinner," which is just awful, when talking about homosexuality or same-sex attraction." A gay male student expressed it this way: "Class discussions are often about how we can love LGBT students, but for some reason, no one who talks in class seems to even know a gay person."

Gay jokes were often heard by respondents, and one gay and celibate male student felt pressured to play along. "A lot of people I live with or close to have very, very close-minded views on homosexuals and if you don't join in on the laughter when jokes come out it automatically is deemed as suspicious." A bisexual alumnus made this statement: "I definitely heard the occasional gay joke. I even remember hearing about some game where the loser had to say, 'I like men,' because that was just shameful." A couple respondents even had their roommates express fear of rooming with someone who was gay. One gay male student remembered, "Before I came out, my suite-mate told me that his worst fear was that housing would put him with a gay student." And a female SSA student experienced something similar.

> I remember during my freshman year having a conversation with my roommate, a hypothetical "Would you get a new roommate if . . . ?" conversation. I asked her, "Would you get a new roommate if I was gay?" Without hesitation, she replied, "Yes." I was shocked and said, "Why?" To which she replied, "I'd be afraid you'd get a crush on me!" I laughed and said, "You're not my type!" I think she still thinks I was kidding.

Interpretive code: Supportive friends. Although a large majority of respondents recalled hurtful comments from their classmates, 56.6 percent of respondents reported having supportive friends ($n = 30$, $N = 53$). Some of these friends who were supportive affirmed same-sex relationships. An SSA female student commented, "I did make a couple of friends in the dorm who are so welcoming and loving that know about me and my friend." The same student continued:

> I think there is the general feeling that because the school appears to stand on one side of the topic of sexuality that students aren't safe to disagree publicly. However, I know that there is a pretty significant group of students, some of which I'm friends with, that do disagree but feel like they must keep their thoughts to themselves or else they'll get in trouble.

A gay male student concurred:

> Regarding my close friends, so far I have told [nine] friends and all have them have been supportive and [eight] out of [nine] of them did not respond awkwardly. . . . Most of them even said they supported me and I would say around half of them have similar views about sexuality.

Other friends of respondents were supportive but did not affirm same-sex relationships. A female SSA student explained,

> I had an excellent experience in my social justice class when a group was presenting the topic of homosexuality because the group was reminding the class that homosexuals are real people, even though they sin. . . . My friends who knew [about my sexuality] took it very well. I think part of the reason for that was because I was choosing not to act on my attractions.

A gay male student reflected on an endearing time with his good friend.

> [My friend] is one of my closest friends, my apartment mate next year, and the second straight person I ever came out to. After saying those two big words, his immediate reaction was to tell me how much he loves me and to give me an awkward—half-sitting hug from the couch across the coffee table.

A male SSA alumnus remarked,

> Every person I came out to at [my school] reacted positively in the sense that they reiterated that they still loved me, though I know

many wouldn't have been supportive had I been in a relationship with another guy. Some of my friends' reactions were positive, accepting and affirming and those people helped me to grow to realize that my same-sex attraction isn't something to be ashamed of.

Several respondents wrote about their friends helping them as they struggled with their same-sex attractions. One gay and celibate male student described his friends this way,

I have talked to friends, in small groups and as individuals and found [support] for my struggles. They have listened and prayed with me. Sometimes we have cried together when I share things that [hurt], and we have found some similarities in struggles.

An SSA student reflected upon his friends, saying,

People that I have told about my [same-sex attractions] have been supportive of my decision to walk away from homosexuality. They have helped me, been [an] ear to listen and shoulder to cry on when I needed to. Overall, the student body seems relatively well-tuned to helping others deal with homosexuality.

Interpretive code: Nudity or joking around. Eighteen of the respondents reported nudity, immodesty, or joking around (34.0 percent, $N = 53$). Nudity and joking around were only reported by male respondents in their dormitories. One male SSA student revealed about his raucous and indecent floor mates, "Often they would run around naked, jump on me naked, get in bed [with] me . . . while naked [for fun]." A gay and celibate male alumnus said, "Some guys would get kinda touchy-feely with each other in a way that was supposed to be funny, but it was incredibly uncomfortable for me." A gay male student recalled,

For me, one of the toughest times in the residence halls was when some athletes did their annual "holiday rounds" when they would walk around in [tight-fitting] underwear and sing Christmas carols to girls. I obviously could avoid seeing this by staying in my room. However, they decided to come to my room and give me the "freshmen of the year" award with a cup that said "mount and dew me."

Another male SSA alumnus described regretfully participating in the humor.

Another issue, looking back, was all the homosexually oriented joking. There was touching, dry humping, jabs, etc., that went on almost every day in the residence halls. I was one who definitely participated in this behavior, but sometimes it did make me uncomfortable.

Participants also recounted instances where floor mates would jokingly expose or rub their genitals on others. One male SSA alumnus wrote,

Men running around naked just for the fun of it, exposing themselves or touching others with their genitals to be funny was not a healthy aspect of that environment for me. I didn't need to look at gay porn. It was walking around in the residence halls.

Another male SSA had a similar experience and indicated how difficult it was for him in the dorms.

Because we are guys, some individuals find it okay to walk around the residence halls in complete nudity or simply flash their genitals. . . . Also one thing that I have [a] very hard time with is the sexual gestures such as grabbing one's buttocks or actually humping another individual. Yes it may be fun, and I put on the face that I take it as a joke. But on the inside my heart is crying and is in pain because they do not understand the struggles that I face.

A male SSA alumnus wrote,

Some RAs choose to condone and encourage behaviors and activities that, I'd label, for lack of a better term, "homoerotic." One of my friends who was a freshman RA last year held a naked slip and slide on his floor for the guys that lived there. From talking to him, it seemed that he wanted to use activities that involved nudity like that to create a close bond as a floor community.

According to this respondent, resident assistants not only permitted nudity as a form of male bonding on the floor, but actually initiated it.

Although nudity on the male dormitory floors seemed to be normative, the examples of nudity above were intentional and done in jest. However, respondents also disclosed their difficulty dealing with the usual dormitory communal bathrooms and community showers. A male SSA student reported,

It was definitely harder last year in the freshman dorm where there were only communal bathrooms. It wasn't uncommon to see guys walking to and from the shower in a towel or just walking around the dorm with their shirts off. The floor I lived on wasn't too "promiscuous," though another floor of the same building was dubbed "the nudist colony."

A bisexual male student disclosed,

> My freshman year dorm had community showers, which proved to be a uniquely uncomfortable experience for me. I was presented with an unprecedented opportunity to see and admire the bodies of some I was sexually attracted to. It was difficult to remain sexually pure within this environment. I often took showers early in the morning or late at night when the room was mostly empty for this reason.

Another male SSA student had a similar experience. "I would wait to take a shower after everyone would leave. I felt uncomfortable around the same sex when I am in the restroom or taking a shower."

All of the examples that involved nudity and joking around were reported by male respondents; however, a few female respondents experienced difficulty in female dormitories. A female SSA alumna depicted a very awkward moment for her.

> In the residence halls, on one of the floors I lived on, it was known as the floor that the girls sat in their bras during floor meetings. One day, I walked on the floor to see all of the girls sitting around in their bras and underwear. I panicked as I got off the elevator and hurried to get to my room. I was not sexually aroused by the sight but was very surprised and uncomfortable.

One lesbian student was asked by her resident assistant not to participate in a floor event because of her same-sex attractions.

> Our female floor has a tradition where we hold a Christmas party before break and we have a secret Santa game, but a lingerie version. After the party everyone tries on their new lingerie and has a dance party. I was told by my RA that the decision was ultimately up to me about whether to attend, but I was strongly encouraged to "sit this one out" because of my attraction, which I did.

A female SSA student divulged, "It was slightly difficult for me to share my room with my immediate roommate because she didn't know that it was hard for me to have her walking around with little clothing on around our room."

Sub-theme: Employees

The second sub-theme consisted of two interpretive codes and seven descriptive codes (see table 4.8). The two interpretive codes were (1) professors and (2) staff. The interpretive codes were explained in order of prevalence, beginning with the first interpretive code with the most responses.

Table 4.8 Sub-theme: Employees

Sub-theme	Interpretive Code	Descriptive Code
Employees	Professors	Anti-gay
		It's a choice
		Supportive
		Welcoming
	Staff	Discipleship
		Offended me
		Safe

Interpretive code: Professors. Twenty-seven respondents provided input on their experiences with professors (50.9 percent, $N = 53$). The researcher discovered that the responses were gathered around two different distribution curves. On one end were responses from students who agreed that God blesses same-sex unions (question C9), thus holding to a PVS. On the other end were responses from students who disagreed that God blesses same-sex unions, thus holding to a TVS. This is consistent with Stratton and colleagues' findings that LGB and SSA students at Christian colleges and universities are not monolithic.[3] Therefore, this interpretive code was divided into positive and negative experiences, and also according to whether respondents held to a PVS or TVS. Nine respondents who held to a PVS wrote about positive experiences with professors. A lesbian student recounted,

> I came out in a paper to one of my most beloved professors. She was supportive and agreed to walk with me on a mutual journey of learning. When the class had a discussion with administration regarding biblical understandings and school policies on the issue of homosexuality, she came to me privately and excused me from class because she knew the discussion might be uncomfortable for me.

A queer male alumnus described,

3. Stratton et al., 21.

> One of the ways I came out my sophomore year was writing an essay titled "Fagnostic: Questions on God and Sexuality," in which I came out and discussed my views and questions as a gay Christian man. It was accepted by both my professor and peer group, which was a great [encouragement] to me.

A male SSA student said, "Most of the faculty, I believe, understand there are different perspectives and that the Christian evangelical circle are debating the issue at hand." Eight respondents who held to a PVS reported negative experiences with their professors. A queer male alumnus made this statement:

> When I wrote a poem based out of my experiences as a queer person and submitted it for peer critique in poetry class, the other students were quite harsh towards it, one of them refusing to be a part of the critique, and the professor confronted me on it outside of the classroom saying that I shouldn't write that type of thing for class. He did tell me that I should write about whatever, but just not for class.

A lesbian student indicated that she received personal harassment from professors. "For other professors, I made sure not to mention it because of their open anti-gay jokes and messages that they discussed in class. I have had many professors make anti-gay jokes both towards me and around me."

Eight respondents who held to a TVS reported positive experiences with professors. A male SSA alumnus commented that his professor gave him hope.

> It was a sociology class and the professor explained that while there is empirical evidence that homosexuality, or even a proclivity toward it, could be genetic, that does not translate to someone being gay. He explained that men who self-identify as gay are gay. Men who have sex with men, or are attracted to men, can self-identify as something else and that that is okay. In an odd way, this gave me hope. In that lecture he shared the story of such a person—a man who had been heavily involved in the gay lifestyle and no longer self-identified as being gay because of his Christian faith.

A female SSA student depicted her professors and the chaplain as being understanding and helpful.

> My professors and the chaplain were incredibly understanding and very helpful. I have one professor who is meeting with me regularly and I can talk about any issues with him. The chaplain

is phenomenal and although it's somewhat awkward he asks great pointed questions to help me prepare myself for the real life outside the bubble of school in regards to my sexual identity.

A gay male student explained,

> [A professor] said that we were confusing gay behavior with being gay. He said that nowhere in the Bible does it say it's a sin to be gay, there are only verses that condemn gay sex. I never really separated these two concepts and what was confusing to me freshman year makes much more sense now that I know and am much more comfortable with my sexual identity.

A male SSA alumnus wrote about "hearing a professor stand up for what Scripture says concerning sexuality when reading relevant Bible passages in the NT, etc. This was positive." Five respondents who held to a TVS reported negative experiences with their professors for different reasons. A bisexual female alumna recalled her professor believing that homosexuality was a choice.

> Some teachers would talk about being gay as if it was a choice and how sinful it was, other teachers were very tactful and gracious about the topic. I believe some of those teachers were naive about there being Christian students who identified that way.

A female SSA student felt her professor viewed LGB and SSA people as less than human.

> Most of what I hear in classes is the whole "homosexuality is just wrong" and "[Gays are] just scraping for proof to make what they do okay." It's more like they are treating homosexuals as a different species that's not human and just act like animals.

A gay and celibate male alumnus remembered how his professor seemed to show little empathy for gays and lesbians.

> My professor said that he didn't see how anyone could read the Bible's statements on sexuality and come to the conclusion that same-sex relationships are acceptable. Now, I agree with that statement, but he said nothing about the personal nature of sexual identity, how it can deeply affect people, how Christians should be open to having a conversation with others to help them deal with their sexual identity. It was just "gay sex is wrong" and nothing else. And it's the "nothing else" part that really bothered me.

A gay male student stated, "I am still working on finding the right interpretation of relevant Scripture, but it does not help when professors cut off the discussion at their points and refuse to engage in [dialogue] about the issue." With all these different perspectives, it is good to be reminded that not all professors are the same as this gay male student illustrated: "My professors are all over the board on the topic."

Interpretive code: Staff. Thirteen respondents provided input on their experiences with staff (24.5 percent, $N = 53$). Similar to experiences with professors, there were four categories divided into positive and negative experiences, and whether respondents held to a TVS or a PVS. Four respondents who held to a TVS commented on positive experiences with staff. A male SSA alumnus praised his resident director:

> The residence life staff was phenomenal. RAs, Area Coordinators (RDs), and the whole staff in Student Life had a restorative approach to discipleship and campus life. . . . My relationship with my RD has continued to this day. She has been very intentional about it, too. I told her of my struggle with homosexuality about a year after I graduated. No one else has ever gone so deep with me in a fully relational way with the intention of building me into a disciple of Christ. Looking back at my time in college, before I realized what I was dealing with, she was discipling and mentoring me through it. Whether she knew or not at the time I am not certain, but she encouraged me in Christ, in my identity, and in [my] calling. Everybody needs someone like her.

Four respondents who held to a PVS also commented on positive experiences with staff. A female SSA student explained, "I was also fortunate enough to have a very relaxed, fairly liberal RD that I could talk to." A queer male alumnus wrote, "My resident director was quite accepting of my decision, even allowing me into student leadership on the condition that I would not enter a same-sex relationship while a student." And a lesbian student reflected, "Our resident director takes great care to ensure that all students, regardless of race, gender, and sexual orientation, feel equally appreciated, welcome, and safe."

Four respondents who held to a PVS reported negative experiences with staff. A gay male student recounted the time when the school found out about his boyfriend.

> My university pastor hands me a copy of the University's policies, and he [had] this part circled under the policy on integrity:

> "Certain sexual behaviors are prohibited. These include, but are not limited to, fornication, adultery, incest and homosexual acts." This sort of offended me, because I felt [as] if he was categorizing me as someone who commits one of those other sins and, I didn't see how my love for an individual could be categorized the same way, regardless of their sex.

Another lesbian student depicted,

> The only issue I ever had within the residence hall was during my coming out process when the resident director heard that I was gay. Because of school rules against "participating in homosexual activity" he was upset and forced me to meet with the dean of students.

A lesbian student said, "My RD was careful in selecting my roommates because she was afraid of there being problems regarding my sexuality." Two respondents who held to a TVS also reported negative experiences with staff. A gay male student described, "There was never any acknowledgment or encouragement from the residence life staff regarding [sexuality] issues beyond heterosexuality. Nor was there any indication that intolerance was not tolerated." There was one gay male student who reported mixed positive and negative responses.

> Coming out to my assistant coach was mixed negative and positive. He was incredibly encouraging, affirming, and hospitable. But in terms of openness and reconciliation, he pressed me back into silence, warning me that others would not be as accepting (including my head coach), even though I had very clearly stated my desires to lead a life of celibate singleness by strength of the Spirit. He hinted of the possibility of me losing my role as team captain and losing respect from my teammates. He also kept repeating the phrase, "Why does it matter?" in what I assumed was an encouraging and inclusive manner intended to break down walls. Ultimately, however, I have come to realize that there is no such thing as inclusive silence.

Sub-theme: Chapels and Student Programming

The third sub-theme consisted of two interpretive codes and thirteen descriptive codes (see table 4.9). The two interpretive codes were (1) sexuality and (2) singleness. Both interpretive codes had the same amount of responses; however, respondents provided more in-depth answers regarding sexuality.

Table 4.9 Sub-theme: Chapels and Student Programming

Sub-theme	Interpretive Code	Descriptive Code
Chapels and student programming	Sexuality	Building bridges Ex-gay speaker Gay marriage is wrong Largely unspoken Not alone Not discussed Restorative Sin
	Singleness	Everybody focused on dating Get married as soon as possible Not helpful Ring by spring Temporary holding period

Interpretive code: Sexuality. Forty-seven respondents provided comments on chapels or student programming that focused on sexuality (88.7 percent, $N = 53$). Thirteen respondents who held to a PVS reported negative chapel and student programming experiences. A lesbian student explained:

> The chapel messages on sexuality simply said that being gay was wrong. We had chapel speakers come in and discuss their "transformation" away from being gay. These messages said that in order to be a Christian you had to turn away from a gay lifestyle and either become straight or single for the rest of their life. The other messages were simply that gays were going to hell and that it was an abomination.

A queer male alumnus wrote, "[A chapel speaker] was quite set on the fact that being a surrendered, redeemed Christian meant that you were living beyond your queer identity and accepting your non-queer identity as a Christian." One gay male student stated, "Most programming on sexuality was heteronormative and assumed every person in the room was straight." "Once a semester, my school would bring in an 'ex-gay' lecturer. Sexuality was talked about in fundamentalist ways," a gay male alumnus recounted. Another gay male alumnus made this statement, "There was one or maybe two chapels in which an [ex-gay] person would come in and talk to us about how they used to be gay, but their faith in God was helping them to overcome it." Seven respondents who held to a TVS also reported negative chapel and student programming experiences. A male SSA student said, "Messages on purity tended to make me feel guilty." A queer male alumnus described,

> There was a chapel about homosexuality. It was basically pro-claimed that it's okay to be gay, you just have to be celibate. I don't think that's helpful, not that celibacy isn't possible. Celibacy just isn't for everyone. How can you preach a sermon that you know isn't going to be considered practical?

"We have an event known as [sex chapel series]. . . . Very rarely do the speakers actually talk about sexuality. Usually, it's just about how we should avoid having sex," a gay and celibate male student reflected. A gay and celibate male alumnus expressed, "The most there was in this category was occasional sermons which would talk about homosexuality as a sin. This was not helpful to me."

Five respondents who held to a PVS reported positive chapel and student programming experiences. A male SSA student remembered, "[A speaker came] to speak on matters of building bridges and dealing more lovingly with our LGBT brothers and sisters." A gay male student conveyed, "During my freshman year, we had a professor speak at chapel with a message that sexuality should be seen as an evolving story instead of rigid definition and that Christians should be the people that make the identification labels." Nine respondents who held to a TVS reported positive chapel and student programming experiences. A gay male student appreciated the chapel on sexuality, but was too scared to focus.

> [A speaker] came for a sexuality chapel series and I appreciated much of what he had to say but don't remember much of what he shared because I was too busy shrinking into my seat feeling like all eyes in the room were crushing me (though I am sure no one had any idea at this point).

A male SSA alumnus was really helped by a chapel on sexuality.

> There was one chapel specifically focused on homosexuality from a restorative, more orthodox, perspective. It gave me the framework to eventually put into words my own struggle with homosexuality and taught me that this was something I was not meant to carry

alone, but in the context of community, no matter how much that freaked me out.

Another male SSA student also appreciated the chapel on sexuality when a speaker came to share about his journey struggling with same-sex attractions. "[The chapel was] very helpful [and] helped me understand that I am not alone in this struggle, I just need to find the courage in myself to reach out for help. [W]hen the time comes I will." A female SSA student recalled,

> [My school] has been amazingly accepting and understanding of sexual minorities, in my opinion. My freshman year was the first year I heard [a speaker] speak in our chapel services. . . . It amazed me that a Christian school would bring in someone who has struggled with homosexuality and makes no claims to have "gone straight" or anything like that. I did not yet realize at that time that I was struggling with something very similar, but the many sexuality-based services have done great things to help this campus understand that homosexuality is not a choice, nor is it the unforgivable sin.

Fifteen respondents indicated that there were no or only one or two chapels or student programming on sexuality during their time in school. One female SSA student confided that even though her school has a committee on sexuality, "I have never been a part of their programming. They often discuss homosexuality, but it makes me nervous to go because for some reason I feel like everyone will then just be able to guess that I'm not normal."

Interpretive code: Singleness. Forty-seven respondents provided comments on chapels or student programming that focused on singleness (88.7 percent, $N = 53$). The majority of respondents ($n = 36$) reflected that there were no chapels or only one chapel focused on singleness. In addition, many respondents expressed how their campus culture greatly encouraged opposite dating. A gay male student provided this excerpt:

> I don't think there is a chapel message or student program that focuses on singleness here on my campus, or at least I don't know of one. There is a phrase here on campus that goes, "Have a ring before spring." So some people believe you find your loved one here, and propose before you graduate from here.

One gay and celibate male student stated,

> The only person who ever spoke about singleness in chapel or as a part of student programming was [a chapel speaker]. Otherwise,

it seems they assume everyone at [my school] will be married by the end of senior year (if not sooner) and talk constantly about marriage.

An asexual female student communicated her frustration this way:

Very few even mention singleness (relative to the numbers focusing on dating/marriage) and when it was presented it was as a "temporary waiting period." Not very helpful. I think there was a total of one series a couple years ago focusing on singleness as a gift and permanent fixture.

A female SSA student wrote:

I was bothered by it not being helpful, since most [of] the speakers who talked about singleness were married. The only one time I heard someone great speak to the all-female chapels, was a lady who spoke about getting [too] close to her mentor. And how easily that mentor one-on-one turned into a more [inappropriate] relationship. She really opened [up] to us, and didn't just talk about feelings of being sad but really informed us all about her experience.

A male SSA alumnus revealed:

[My school] exhibits a strong marital culture ("ring by spring," "Mrs. degrees") that is typical of Evangelical Christian universities. I never once heard a chapel message or student program on singleness. Had I experienced that I suspect it wouldn't have had a strong effect on me (I really want to fall in love and get married someday).

A male SSA student: "There aren't many that focus on singleness. Most everyone here is wanting to get married as soon as possible."

Summary: Experiences (Overarching Theme)

There were six major findings that emerged from the overarching theme of experiences. First, respondents reported both positive and negative experiences. Second, respondents reported that classmates (1) were hurtful with their comments; (2) were supportive; or (3) joked around through nudity and immodesty. Third, respondents who held to a PVS generally reported positive experiences with employees who held to a PVS and negative experiences with employees who held to a TVS. Fourth, respondents who held to a TVS generally reported positive experiences with employees who helped them live out a traditional sexual ethic and negative experiences with employees who had little compassion for those with same-sex attractions. Fifth, respondents generally reported positive or negative chapel experiences according to whether the speaker agreed with their own sexual ethic. However, some respondents who held to a TVS did report that the chapels on sexuality only focused on morality and not upon pastoral care of SSA individuals. Sixth, the majority of respondents reported that singleness was not mentioned enough or not mentioned at all in chapels or student programming.

Overarching Theme: Recommendations

The third overarching theme emerged from four sub-themes, twelve interpretive codes, and seventy-three descriptive codes. Fifty-nine respondents provided answers that fell into this overarching theme ($N = 59$). The four sub-themes were: (1) institutional policies; (2) campus climate; (3) programming; and (4) groups and mentoring. When creating narrative codes for this overarching theme of recommendations, priority was not necessarily placed upon finding common meanings among descriptive codes, and outlying descriptive codes were not necessarily ignored. In some instances, one or two respondents provided a very insightful recommendation that no one else had mentioned. These insightful recommendations were given priority, even though there was low prevalence among more common descriptive codes. Some interpretive codes within this last overarching theme may not have as much representation within each sub-theme and may not have been recommended by other respondents. Therefore, interpretive codes were not created based upon repeated recommendations among respondents. Rather, interpretive codes were created based upon its creativeness.

Sub-theme: Institutional Policies

The first sub-theme consisted of two interpretive codes and seventeen descriptive codes (see table 4.10). The two interpretive codes were (1) disagree and (2) agree. The interpretive codes are explained below.

Table 4.10 Sub-theme: Institutional Policies

Sub-theme	Interpretive Code	Descriptive Code
Institutional policies	Disagree	Don't categorize Double standard Love isn't sin Misinterpreted Non-discrimination Outdated Singling out Take out portions of policies Vague
	Agree	Be consistent Bible is clear Distinguish between orientation and behavior Having standards in place Holding me accountable Orthodox interpretation Provide parameters Submit to authority

Interpretive code: Disagree. Thirty-two respondents disagreed with the institutional policies (54.2 percent, $N = 59$). All respondents who disagreed with the institutional policies either agreed or somewhat agreed that God blesses same-sex unions (question C9). Several advocated for the removal of the statements against homosexuality. A female SSA alumna challenged: "Take out all 'hate' language in school policy. A statement that encourages safety and acceptance in school paperwork would be nice as well." A bisexual male student retorted:

> The fact that the covenant singles out homosexual relationships is a bit ludicrous. It is 2013, for God's sake. . . . I understand [my school's] stance on sex outside marriage. That, I can live with. I cannot live with the singling out of homosexual behavior in the [lifestyle agreement].

Other respondents disagreed with how the school interpreted the Bible. One lesbian alumna wrote, "It relies on proof texting and proscriptive gender 'norms' that are outdated and don't take into account the loving side of God for creation." A bisexual male student made this statement:

> I feel that biblical issues with LGBT lifestyles have been misinter-preted and their importance has been overstated. My university maintains the fundamentalist evangelical viewpoint that they are sinful. There's a clear mismatch in our points of view. . . . I don't ask that the administration change their own personal viewpoints on the issue. But I would love to see them recognize that it's very much not a black-and-white issue, and that their personal view-points should stay personal.

A queer male alumnus explained:

> I disagree with what it was because I think that the Bible is not clear enough on the ethics of minority sexuality for us to draw conclusive statements about it. We have to just allow people to fol-low God and let him lead them where he wants to, whether that is into a single life, or a straight or queer relationship.

A gay male student reasoned:

> I think that this is enforcing one view of an interpretation of the Bible on people who might not agree with that interpretation. There is a small but significant minority of Christians who believe that it is acceptable to be gay and Christian, and this law does not take those students' beliefs into account.

One female SSA student believed that the school should protect LGB and SSA students from discrimination by putting sexual identity into the non-discrimination clause. "How can sexual orientation be excluded from the non-discrimination statement, but [my school] still be considered a safe place that reflects Christ's love for all students?" Another gay male student stated that he believed this was a human rights issue. "I don't agree with the university's statement on homosexuality due [to the] fact that it is a double standard on human rights. Those that are homosexual cannot have a relation-ship, while those that are heterosexual can." And a female alumna conveyed, "Don't call love a sin. It's incredibly degrading and offensive and untrue to the roots of compassion that Christianity attempts to grow in its followers."

Some respondents disagreed with same-sex sexual practice being compared to other sins. A gay male student expressed, "They put us in the same category as someone who is an adulterer, fornicator, or someone who is into incest." Another gay male student concurred: "Do not categorize homosexuality with bestiality, adultery, incest, etc." Respondents also complained that the policies needed clarification. One gay male student described: "It is vague. It just says that homosexual behavior is prohibited. Does that mean just sex? Or can I date on campus? Kiss a guy? Yet if it were more clear I would feel only more attacked and discriminated by it." A bisexual female student argued that her school should allow a gay couple to hold hands and kiss on campus.

> While I believe that two Christians in a relationship should maintain a standard of purity, any homosexual behavior at my university is against our Community Covenant, which all students must sign. Therefore, even holding hands or cuddling or kissing is against the standard in the [lifestyle agreement] for homosexuals or bisexuals. It is approved for heterosexual couples, and they walk around campus holding hands and you see many of them kissing on campus.

Although there was one gay and celibate male alumnus who believed that gay relationships are not blessed by God and are sinful, he only somewhat agreed with the lifestyle agreement. "I am less convinced that it is particularly wise to attempt to legislate sexual ethics through lifestyle agreements."

Interpretive code: Agree. Nineteen respondents agreed with the institutional policies (32.2 percent, $N = 59$), but many suggested ways in which the school could improve. One male SSA student somewhat agreed with the statement for this reason.

> I didn't wholeheartedly agree with it. Because it does [not] have an amnesty policy if you ask for help, or if you are willing to accept help if confronted. But I feel it is more "to address the problem" rather than to "know the person."

A gay and celibate male alumnus suggested that the school should be more consistent with discipline.

> I agree with the letter of the statement. But as it's carried out, I feel like homosexuality was definitely singled out way more than heterosexually equivalent sins. There was a lot of sexual sin going on, and at my school there was a lot more pressure on people who messed up sexually as homosexuals. Basically enforcement was stricter on gay things, though the letter of the agreement was just as hard on heterosexuals who weren't married. So my problem is the enforcement, not the actual agreement.

Several respondents reported that their school policies against same-sex sexual practice could be easily misunderstood. One gay and celibate student wrote, "Change the covenants to be more clear on the issue. It is an easy area to be vague about." Another female SSA student agreed: "I think one thing would be to make it clearer in the lifestyle agreement that it is activity that is prohibited, not just attractions." Another gay and celibate male alumnus addressed how his school recently made a change to clarify the statement on same-sex sexual practice.

> [My school] recently updated their statement on human sexuality. In the update, they included a distinction between sexual orientation and sexual behavior. "The former pertains to attraction or desire, which are not necessarily under a person's control," while sexual behavior is under someone's control. That addition was incredibly encouraging for me because it made me feel like the institution shared my perspective concerning sexual identity. I don't believe that I can control who I am attracted to, but I can control what I do with that attraction. Therefore, I am no different from a heterosexual student with regards to this statement.

Participants also desired a pastoral aspect to be included in the institutional policies. A male SSA student suggested, "Create a biblical and compassionate position on the issue and make that available as well." A gay and celibate male alumnus summarized his suggestion this way:

> I think it would be great if faculty and administrators can demonstrate the institution's commitment to helping sexual minority students and aiding them in dealing with their sexual identity. Institutional statements can often be misunderstood, and I think it's important for the faculty and administration to bring clarity to those statements and those policies. Rather than focusing on a list of things that you shouldn't do or things that you can't do, the university should focus on coming around sexual minority students in a loving community that allows them to deal with their identity as a sexual minority without overemphasizing the rules and regulations.

Another gay and celibate male student said, "They say they agree with heterosexuality but don't mention anything that may help those dealing with same-sex attraction."

Several participants wholeheartedly agreed with the institutional policies forbidding same-sex sexual practice and did not want the school to change. A male SSA alumnus said, "I believe our statement on homosexuality was woven into the overarching language of sexuality so as not to focus solely on one temptation over others." A bisexual male student remarked, "I agree with my school's statement that we are not, as followers of Christ, to practice homosexuality, because I find the Bible to be very clear on that." A female SSA student communicated,

> Our statement recognizes homosexual behavior as a sin, not the mere presence of same-sex attraction. I feel like this is biblically correct because all of the passages in Scripture condemning homosexuality to me sound like they are condemning the behavior.

Another male SSA alumnus agreed: "If we submit to the authority of Jesus, then what the Bible says is what we must follow." A gay male student indicated his willingness to be held accountable by his school. "I believe that homosexual acts are a sin, so I don't have a problem with [my school] holding me accountable to the Bible." A male SSA student reflected on his reason for selecting an institution of Christian higher education.

> Although I may be attracted to the same sex, I am glad that I chose a Christian university because the struggle to remain firm in my faith and overcome such a temptation would be intensified to a greater degree compared [to] if I attended a public academic institution. By having these standards in place, it reminds me of the lifestyle that glorifies God. As a believer I hope to glorify God in all the things that I do. By not being open about my homosexuality, it allows me to foster that I must suppress such feelings and the temptations so that I may grow in God more.

One female SSA alumna disclosed:

> Because I knew what the expectations were in my college on maintaining biblical sexual purity (on all levels), I was more than willing to agree with the statement and I had no intentions of acting out on my temptations for the same gender. Since I hadn't acted out before then, my plan was to not to.

A male SSA student reported:

> [My school's lifestyle agreement] prohibits homosexual activity, and I think this is good since the purpose of the covenant is to provide parameters for a healthy, godly community and since engaging in those relationships are both unbiblical and detrimental to those involved.

Another male SSA alumnus exhorted his school: "I really do believe with my whole heart that Christian schools need not depart from an orthodox interpretation of Scripture and Christian tradition." A male SSA alumnus encouraged his school: "Whatever the case, though, don't give in to the world's pressure of making homosexuality normal."

Sub-theme: Campus Climate

The second sub-theme consisted of four interpretive codes and twenty-seven descriptive codes (see table 4.11). The four interpretive codes were: (1) awareness and attitudes; (2) hurtful comments; (3) nudity and immodesty; and (4) singleness. The interpretive codes are explained in order of prevalence.

Table 4.11 Sub-theme: Campus Climate

Sub-theme	Interpretive Code	Descriptive Code
Campus climate	Awareness and attitudes	Compassion
		Love
		No worse
		Not more severe
		Not singled out
		Not super sin
		Raise awareness
		Support
		There are others
		Understanding
		Welcoming
	Hurtful comments	Careful what you say
		Cruel remarks
		Derogatory remarks
		Gay jokes
		Slurs
		That's so gay
		Words matter

	Nudity and immodesty	Community bathrooms Flashing Immodesty Naked Privacy Public nudity
	Singleness	Honor celibate singles Less emphasis on dating and marriage Less pressure on pursuing relationships

Interpretive code: Awareness and attitudes. More than half of the respondents provided recommendations on awareness and attitudes (59.3 percent, $n = 35$, $N = 59$). These were general comments for people to be more loving and supportive, to raise awareness, and to understand that homosexuality is not the worst sin. One bisexual male student explained:

> I agree with my school's statement that we are not, as followers of Christ, to practice homosexuality, because I find the Bible to be very clear on that. However, I would like to see a more loving attitude by the student body toward those who do have same-sex attractions, and I would like to see them develop an ability to hate the sin, but love the sinner. I don't mean only at a skin-deep level, but at a level that shows genuine compassion and understanding, and a willingness to help.

An asexual female alumna reflected on the desire of some to want to point out others' faults. "Maybe taking it upon themselves less to offer correction—people often use the defense that you're supposed to correct in love, and/or [not] tolerate sin, but regardless there's a distinct lack of empathy." A gay male student encouraged students to put themselves in the shoes of LGB and SSA people.

> Understand that this is a subject no one wants to lose friendships over. Think of the deepest darkest thing you have done or feel and ask yourself why you don't tell anyone about it and talk about it freely. We all want to be accepted but if we are intimate about everything then we will all feel better. [Instead] of judging characteristics, meet them face-to-face and learn more about them. Try to feel what they feel. Try to understand them and love them. Also, understand that you will never fully understand and give grace!

A male SSA alumnus hoped that Christian colleges and universities could be more welcoming.

> Christian universities and the church at large ought to be known as a place where you don't have to fix yourself up to be welcomed in with open arms, with no qualifications, with no questions about whether [you're] "gay" or "straight." Love ought to come first. Sadly that's not the reality of those places, but it can be.

Another male SSA alumnus stated, "Love them like Christ loved humanity, remove the plank from their own eye first, and don't treat sexual minority students as if their sin issue is their identity. Include, don't marginalize them."

There was a desire to raise awareness on the campuses of Christian colleges and universities. A male SSA student viewed it this way: "Simply attempt to raise awareness in [the] residence halls. [Straight] guys don't think that what they do is a problem." One gay and celibate male alumnus reported, "Understand that we are Christians and we are not heterosexual. 'Christian' and 'non-heterosexual' [are] not mutually exclusive, but [it] often feels as if many people think that." Respondents wanted their classmates also to know that LGB and SSA students are on campus. A gay and celibate male alumnus made this comment: "College and university students need to know that there are other Christian students who are struggling with their sexual identity and that the Christian community must come around those people to help them." And a queer male alumnus wrote, "Allow your peers to define themselves how they want and respect that. I was constantly [relabeled] as 'struggling with homosexuality' rather than how I self-identified as gay. It was grating and demeaning."

Several respondents wanted their classmates to understand that same-sex sexual practice was not the worst sin. One male SSA student indicated this with his statement, "I agree that they should not encourage this [behavior]. What really upsets me is that they treat homosexual sin as more severe then heterosexual sin. [This is] not acceptable." A male bisexual student exhorted his classmates: "Help the students understand that while it is a sin, it is in the same level as heterosexual sin, and it cannot be treated like the be-all end-all super sin that condemns a person without forgiveness." A female asexual alumna said,

> In discussions of non-heterosexuality, if we/they really believe that it is a sin no worse than any other sin, it would be good to

demonstrate that—focus on other issues, even non-hot-topic ones. People get so caught up in the idea of homosexuality, the "big issue."

A gay and celibate male alumnus concurred: "Homosexuality should never be singled out and treated differently. We feel differently enough already."

Interpretive code: Hurtful comments. Seventeen respondents gave recommendations in relation to eliminating hurtful comments (28.8 percent, $N = 59$). A bisexual female alumna conveyed: "Be careful with what you say. Yes, it's a Christian environment, but even Christians are homosexual and a person does not always know who they are." A male SSA student made this statement: "Don't say stupid, mindless comments. It hurts more than you could ever know." One gay and celibate male alumnus recommended: "College students need to understand that we are real people, and the culture that is perpetuated by using the gay community as a [punch line] is hurtful and damaging. Poorly timed or poorly placed comments can have a profound impact." A gay male student wrote, "Make it clear at the beginning of the year that there will be no tolerance of harassment or hate-speech." Another gay male student expressed this: "When you say 'that's gay' or when you make other jokes you might be unintentionally hurting someone else." A gay and celibate male student communicated, "Crude jokes are even [covered] in [my school's] lifestyle agreement. . . . Yet crude humor is never [addressed] in the halls. Sometimes it even seems encouraged." A female SSA student explained:

> I want you to know that words matter. You may think that you are just vocalizing your view of what Scripture says is right, but there's a side you don't see. You may not expect this, but I also think that homosexual activity is wrong. Just so you're aware, calling my unchosen feelings disgusting and despicable doesn't make it any easier for me to follow God's law. I don't like that I have the feelings either, but they don't just go away because it's wrong for me to act on them.

Interpretive code: Nudity and immodesty. Seven respondents gave recommendations in relation to nudity and immodesty in the dormitories (11.9 percent, $N = 59$). All the respondents were male. A male SSA student encouraged men in the dorms, "Try to [understand that] when they jump on someone that struggles with same-sex attraction when they are naked, it is just like [if] a naked girl were to jump on them. They just don't think about all that." One male SSA alumnus provided this recommendation: "Don't flaunt your naked body in the residence halls to be funny." A male SSA student suggested,

> Flashing and public nudity in the residence halls should not be allowed because it really intensifies the struggle for other individuals who try to suppress such emotions and try to keep this a secret. In the guy residence halls, make it clear that each resident is to respect each other's body and not hump or touch inappropriate areas of other residents.

A gay male student remarked, "Be conscious of your own modesty. I think it's much [easier] for guys to be immodest than girls and that makes it harder for gay men." One gay and celibate male alumnus indicated the importance of privacy.

> The younger generation already wants more privacy in their living spaces, so in development of living space for students this would be good to pursue. It would help sexual minority students, too. Going through my sexual peak in a dorm full of naked and half naked guys was so difficult. It's like a straight man who is required to live with, bathe with, dress in front of, and wrestle with a bunch of beautiful young female college students. It's so uncomfortable.

Another gay male student agreed. "Make sure students in the residence halls can have adequate privacy, especially in dorm rooms and bathrooms." A male SSA student advised eliminating community bathrooms. "When constructing new dorms, staying away from community bathrooms would obviously be helpful."

Interpretive code: Singleness. Three respondents gave recommendations in relation to emphasizing singleness (5.1 percent, $N = 59$). A female SSA student wrote, "We also need to quit making jokes about and putting so much emphasis on dating and marriage." A male SSA student explained:

> I would encourage them to create less overall pressure on pursuing relationships. When going out with friends or hosting other activities, they can be mindful of creating an atmosphere that is friendly to both couples and singles. Also, couples can be considerate of others in a group by not focusing exclusively on each other but rather balancing their time with each other and other friends.

One gay and celibate male alumnus suggested:

It would also be quite useful if the school honored celibate singles of all orientations and didn't focus so much on a culture of marriage. Marriage is important, and most people do it, but many Christians act in such a way that makes me think that Paul the apostle would have felt left out.

A couple respondents provided some interesting recommendations that did not fit into any of the other interpretive codes. One gay male alumnus wrote, "I also don't think they should make the sexual minority their 'evangelism project.' Sometimes, I thought that men were becoming my friends just so they could heterosexualize me." Another gay and celibate male alumnus suggested, "Perhaps having an ombudsperson or some specific place gay students could go to talk about issues would be good."

Sub-theme: Programming

The third sub-theme consisted of three interpretive codes and fifteen descriptive codes (see table 4.12). The three interpretive codes were: (1) inform and train; (2) consider other interpretations; and (3) singleness. The interpretive codes are explained in order of prevalence, beginning with the first interpretive code with the most responses.

Table 4.12 Sub-theme: Programming

Sub-theme	Interpretive Code	Descriptive Code
Programming	Inform and train	Awareness Education More understanding Orientation Outside sources Panel discussions Safe dialogue Sensitivity training Share stories
	Consider other interpretations	Both sides Different viewpoints Diversity in theology Open minded
	Singleness	Celibacy Singleness

Interpretive code: Inform and train. Twenty-eight respondents indicated recommendations for informing students and training staff (47.5 percent, $N = 59$). Students needed to be informed and educated on LGB issues. A bisexual male student reported: "I would say that my school needs to develop a program to help other students understand homosexuality from both a biblical and psychological perspective." A female SSA student suggested:

> Educate students. Some are so sheltered and have this knee-jerk reaction to judge those who struggle with homosexuality. They'd never admit it, but it's obvious. We need to get this out in the open so it stops being seen as so much worse than other sins.

A gay male alumnus remarked that the school's administration should give students more freedom.

> Continue to demonstrate to students that you are willing to engage the conversation in a loving manner, letting the student body lead talks and conversation without administrative involvement, showing students that they trust their direction and understanding of the topic. Faculty and administration can continue to build LGBTQ+ issues into their diversity and sensitivity training.

A lesbian student wrote about informing students at the beginning of the year.

> I think that there should be a sexuality panel (along with topics like race, faith, differing gender identity, etc.) at the beginning of the year. Students should know what language will and will not be tolerated, how to respect others, and where to find support or guidance with these topics, whether they identify as SSA or feel uncomfortable with this topic.

Another lesbian alumna encouraged sensitivity training for all students.

> Sensitivity training so people don't assume LGBT students will be attracted to them simply due to being same sex. Just a myth-busting session in an orientation week would do worlds of good. . . . Include mandatory sessions during summer/pre-start orientation that contain inclusive information and vocabulary, information on GSA groups on-campus, and resources for students and families.

A male SSA alumnus recalled his school allowing LGB and SSA students to tell their personal stories.

> I'm thrilled that while I attended [my school] there was a night simply dedicated to letting LGBT members of the community share their stories. No debate, no arguments, no potentially misinterpreted Bible verses. Just the people in power ("heterosexuals") listening to those who are sexual minorities. Events like that need to happen more often.

A male SSA alumnus challenged schools to hold up the TVS with compassion.

> Continue to provide safe places of dialogue on campus and in chapel where the biblical stance of heterosexuality [as] God's norm is upheld, but grace and a lack of harsh judgment and deep understanding is portrayed. . . . Also, having those safe forums of interaction will help, and having the leaders demonstrate Christ-like love to all students, which will hopefully then be demonstrated to sexual minority students. It starts at the top with the leadership and faculty.

A male SSA student expressed, "Don't be afraid to talk about the issue."

Respondents suggested that there should be training for staff. A female SSA student reflected, "I was really shocked that during my RA training there was no session dedicated to talking about sexuality." A male SSA alumnus commented:

> I would have loved to have seen a training component for resident assistants that better explained the university's stance on homosexuality and how to walk alongside someone who opens up to you—and how to make sure you set yourself up as a safe person someone can talk to.

A gay male student had this message for residence life staff.

> Education is vital. Make sure you are completely aware of how best to support LGBT students living in your housing and on your campus. Get outside of your own understanding and experience and feel the daily marginalization they feel. Be open, be loving.

A gay male alumnus said,

> I think [my school's residence life] staff should continue to engage outside sources for direction . . . so that outside viewpoints and those that have formerly experienced discrimination can give ideas about how to make the residence halls safer.

Interpretive code: Consider other interpretations. Ten respondents indicated recommendations to consider other interpretations (16.9 percent, N = 59). A pansexual transgender female student indicated,

> There are many ways to interpret the Bible. There are millions of interpretations concerning the Bible. All Christians must live in harmony with these interpretations. Therefore a Christian university should make its position clear, but it should not enforce extra dating/physical restrictions on minority students.

A lesbian student reported:

> I think it would be helpful for the administration to welcome different viewpoints [other] than their own. I do not want to hear from only Christians who are ex-gay or who are gay and celibate. . . . This variety of viewpoints seems more respectful because it assumes that we are adults who are capable of making our own decisions about our faith. I do not want to be "protected" from different viewpoints or force-fed whatever the college wants me to believe.

A male SSA student made this statement:

> I believe it is time for Christian colleges to start bringing all sides of the conversation together and discuss the matter of sexuality, in general, and begin to carve a Christian approach to dealing with homosexuality, singleness, marriage, and what can and cannot be accepted.

A gay male student stated:

> Allow for more diversity in thought and theology. Allow for questions and complexities. It is not helpful [to fill] students with shame and guilt and make them feel like an other by pinning them down with a conservative theology. Encourage them to think on their own because, after all, you are an educational [institution] of higher learning which should [help] to promote critical thinking.

A male SSA student wrote, "To begin presenting the other views on Christian living a little more forcefully." A bisexual male student desired openness but wanted people to still maintain a TVS. "Make sure they allow open dialogue from both sides, and allow people to share the biblical view on homosexuality."

Interpretive code: Singleness. Two respondents indicated recommendations for placing more value on singleness and celibacy (3.4 percent, N = 59). A female SSA alumna suggested:

I would have loved to have heard about the value of singleness or what [you] do when you don't "feel attracted" to the opposite gender. Marriage was discussed a lot, but not so much about being holy in your sexuality whether you marry or not. It seemed as if marriage was better than being single. And in some ways, it was pushed rather than waiting. For someone like me that struggled with same-sex attraction, it was implied that getting married would "fix" my sexual brokenness. This message was a lie communicated to many of us students as we sat in the classrooms.

Another female SSA student explained that she would like to have seen "more chapel or programming on celibacy or sexual minority [issues]."

Sub-theme: Groups and Mentoring

The fourth sub-theme consisted of three interpretive codes and fourteen descriptive codes (see table 4.13). The three interpretive codes were (1) support groups, (2) advocacy groups, and (3) mentoring. The interpretive codes are explained in order of prevalence, beginning with the first interpretive code with the most responses.

Table 4.13 Sub-theme: Groups and Mentoring

Sub-theme	Interpretive Code	Descriptive Code
Groups and mentoring	Support groups	Discipleship Find courage No different than others Private group Process my issues Safe place Voice their feelings
	Advocacy groups	Equality group Gay Straight Alliance LGBT mentors Safe space Welcoming
	Mentoring	Mentoring One-on-one

Interpretive code: Support groups. Sixteen respondents recommended support groups for those who are SSA (27.1 percent, $N = 59$). A male SSA student made this statement, "Encourage [students] that struggle with same-sex attraction to understand that what they are [struggling with] is no different than what [others] struggle with." One bisexual male student made this statement: "Allow struggling students . . . to voice their feelings as well. We have to maintain a biblical stance without casting stones and hurting those we mean to help." A female SSA student agreed. "School ought to be a safe place to struggle and be refined by Christ, but that can never happen if there is a constant need to hide." A male SSA student reported: "One thing I love about [my school] and would recommend for other colleges is the discipleship group they offer for students who struggle with homosexuality. This creates a safe place for them to encourage and sharpen each other." However, a gay and celibate male student indicated his fear of going to a support group.

> We also need to respect that not everyone wants to be outed, and most of us are very sensitive about who we tell about it. Thus, small groups or discussions on the issue are hard for me to go to because I feel like everyone will know that I'm gay because I'm going to this meeting.

And another male SSA student concurred. "[It is] helpful to know that there is such a support group out there, but I seem to not find the courage to go, and maybe a little shame to open up about such issues." This female SSA student suggested an alternative option with a private online group.

> Maybe open a blog or something where it's a private group, [for] only those who struggle with homosexuality. It doesn't have to be a blog, but perhaps a group meeting. Where they would discuss their issues and sins. They wouldn't personally have to say, but make it more of [an] anonymous type thing. Also, it must be talked about because if it isn't they already feel like they are alone. And we need to help them through. If they do want help, that is.

A female SSA student said that a support group would have helped her work through her issues in a healthy way.

> I would have been more engaged and honest about where I really was if a group was offered for those who wanted to process about their sexuality issues or same-sex attraction. . . . Offer opportunities for students who are grappling with their sexuality (porn watching, [fantasies], etc.) and same-sex attractions to discuss

these things in a safe environment such as a support group or mentoring.

In hindsight, she realized that the risk of others knowing about her struggle would have been worth it.

Interpretive code: Advocacy groups. Fourteen respondents recommended their schools to have LGB advocacy groups (23.7 percent, $N = 59$). A female SSA alumna wrote,

> [People should be] accepting and respecting all sexual orientations. A good start would be to have an equality group allowed on campus. I'm not saying that [my school] has to have a gay pride parade every semester, but treating all sexual orientations with the same level of respect and dignity should be mandatory.

A lesbian former student recounted her attempts to start something on her campus. "I tried multiple times to institute a group/safe space in coordination with the counseling center on campus, but did not receive much affirmation [during] the time I was there." A lesbian alumna said,

> Establish a GSA that doesn't judge its members or require reparative therapy-style counseling for people who come out. Accept everyone and engender a [non-judgmental] social environment on campus. . . . A mentor group of older GLBT students would be a good idea not only to welcome incoming students to the campus and surrounding community, but they could provide feedback and ideas to school administration about the inclusiveness of the campus environment.

A gay male student made this suggestion:

> I feel that having something for the LGBT community to connect on campus would be great and overall beneficial. I feel like if we had a GSA or something of the sort, it would not only allow people to be more informed, but also would allow people of the LGBT community somewhere to go to connect with each other in a safe welcoming place.

A gay male student communicated: "Make institutionalized groups to support these students. Not just therapy groups, but social ones that provide safe places for students of similar experience to gather and feel united." A lesbian student wrote about her desire to integrate her sexuality and her faith. "I also feel that they should create an environment in which gay and lesbian students are allowed to discuss their sexuality in light of their faith."

Interpretive code: Mentoring. Three respondents recommended that their schools create mentoring opportunities for LGB and SSA students (5.1 percent, $N = 59$). A male SSA student reported: "[I] strongly encourage one-on-one student/[professor] mentoring [with] safe individuals that understand." A bisexual female alumna suggested that, even though she was not open about her sexuality, she wished that she had been open and had sought out a mentor.

> I did not admit to myself or anyone that I identified myself as a bisexual woman until my last year at college and I believe that if I would have been able to sooner I could have been able to search this out with a mentor and be able really [to] know what that all [meant].

A male SSA student was glad that his school offered mentoring possibilities. "[My school] encourages mentor relationships and resident hall Bible studies, which can be helpful."

Summary: Recommendations (Overarching Theme)

There were five major findings that emerged from the overarching theme of recommendations. First, respondents who held to a PVS wanted the institutional policies against same-sex sexual practice to be removed, while respondents who held to a TVS did not want the institutional policies to be changed to affirm same-sex sexual practice. Second, respondents reported that the institutional policies were easily misunderstood and were not applied consistently. Third, respondents provided recommendations to improve campus climate by: (1) raising awareness and improving attitudes; (2) reducing hurtful comments; (3) reducing nudity and immodesty in the dorms; and (4) honoring celibate singles. Fourth, respondents suggested improvements regarding programming by: (1) informing and training through awareness and sensitivity training; (2) considering other interpretations; and (3) affirming celibacy and singleness. Fifth, respondents recommended support groups, advocacy groups, and mentoring opportunities.

$$-\ 5\ -$$

Evaluation and Discussion

Synthesis and Integration of Findings

THE PROBLEM THIS PROJECT addressed was the sense of marginalization experienced by LGB and SSA Christian college and university students. The research purpose for this present study was to influence change and improvement of the campus climate at Christian colleges and universities for LGB and SSA students. There were two research questions. The first research question was: What are the experiences of Christian college or university LGB and SSA students? The second research question was: How can the campus climate at Christian colleges and universities be less marginalizing for LGB and SSA students? The two research questions provided a framework for the synthesis of the findings that emerged from chapter 4. In addition, the researcher drew together the three primary data sources into a set of integrated conclusions. The three data sources were: (1) biblical-theological reflection; (2) related literature; and (3) data from this field research. The review of related literature can be found in Appendix E.

Conclusions Related to Experiences

The first research question was related to the experiences of Christian college or university LGB and SSA students. There were six conclusions related to the experiences of the respondents. First, there was diversity among respondents in the way they identified their own sexuality, in their views related to the morality of same-sex relationships, and in their agreement with institutional policies on same-sex sexual practice. Therefore, it should not be assumed that all LGB and SSA students identify as being gay, disagree with the TVS, or are pursuing gay relationships. This was consistent with the findings of Stratton and colleagues that LGB and SSA students at Christian colleges and universities are not monolithic in their attitudes about sexuality.[1] Although LGB and SSA students and alumni in disagreement with their school may be more vocal, those in agreement with their school may be less vocal. Yarhouse discovered that, among LGB and SSA people, there were some who were "assertive advocates" and some who were "sincere strugglers."[2] Assertive advocates were LGB and SSA Christians who advocate "for a change in Christian doctrine about sexuality and sexual behavior." Sincere strugglers were LGB and SSA Christians who genuinely try "to live faithfully before God with their sexuality . . . [and] agree with traditional Christian doctrine about sexuality and sexual behavior."[3] Although Yarhouse describes these two types of LGB and SSA people, it is very likely that this is not a dichotomy, but rather a spectrum. The researcher believes that students may fall anywhere along this spectrum from assertive advocate to sincere struggler, or anywhere in between. In addition, students may move along this spectrum during their time as students. During college years, students are finding their own personal identity, and that often, if not always, changes during these formative years. Therefore, while addressing LGB and SSA students, administrators, staff, and faculty at Christian colleges and universities should not treat them as simply one group but as individuals on a continuum and on a journey.

Second, respondents generally felt lonely as LGB or SSA Christian college or university students. The respondents on average scored between "sometimes" or "often" for feeling a lack of companionship, left out, or isolated. Just as the sojourner, the widow, and the orphan were unimportant and social outcasts, LGB and SSA students at Christian colleges and universities reported feeling unimportant, as if they too were social outcasts. There are two reasons why administrators, staff, and faculty at Christian colleges and universities should seek ways to reduce marginalization of LGB and SSA students. The first reason is the biblical mandate to care for

1. Stratton et al., 21.
2. Yarhouse, *Homosexuality*, 158.
3. Yarhouse, *Homosexuality*, 158.

the marginalized. The second reason is that all students on Christian college and university campuses should have equal opportunity to grow intellectually and spiritually. But if LGB and SSA students feel marginalized, this can hinder their education and their journey of faith.

Third, respondents generally sensed a need to hide their sexuality. This was consistent with the related research from both secular colleges and universities[4] and Christian colleges and universities.[5] In spite of secular institutions not having institutional policies against same-sex sexual practice and not being Christian institutions, LGB and SSA students still felt a need to hide their sexuality. This feeling was not unique to Christian colleges and universities and the absence of institutional policies did not reveal an absence of this phenomenon. See Appendix E (literature review) for more details. However, no available research had asked why LGB and SSA students felt the need to hide their sexuality. Therefore, this was the first research to ask the respondents why they felt a need to hide their sexuality. Respondents felt a need to hide their sexuality because of (1) fear of others' response; (2) negative climate; (3) lack of readiness; and (4) fear of disciplinary action. Some respondents felt able to be open about their sexuality because of (1) trustworthy and supportive friends; (2) a sense of being comfortable with their sexuality; (3) a desire to help others as an advocate or as a struggler; and (4) a desire to help themselves. Although respondents felt the need to hide their sexuality, several expressed that they wish they could have been more open.

Fourth, respondents reported a negative campus climate. This was overwhelmingly consistent with the related research literature on secular campuses[6] and Christian campuses.[7] In spite of secular institutions not having institutional policies against same-sex sexual practice and not being Christian institutions, LGB and SSA students still reported a negative campus climate—sometimes even in the most gay friendly campuses in the nation. The report of a negative campus climate was not unique to Christian colleges and universities and the absence of institutional policies did not reveal an absence of this phenomenon. See Appendix E (literature review)

4. Rankin, *Campus Climate*, 24; Brown et al., "Report," 10.

5. Wentz and Wessel, 46; Yarhouse et al., "Listening to Sexual Minorities," 101–2; Stratton et al., 19.

6. Rankin, *Campus Climate*, 4; Brown et al., "Report," 9; Longerbeam et al., 225; Silverschanz et al., 185; Rankin et al., *2010 State*, 9.

7. Wentz and Wessel, 45; Yarhouse et al., "Listening to Sexual Minorities," 104.

for more details. Respondents perceived their campus climate to be negative because of (1) hurtful comments; (2) nudity and joking around in the dorms; and (3) a strong opposite-sex dating emphasis among students. The hurtful comments were mostly "ambient" (and not "personal") comments from other students. This was consistent with the findings from Rankin's 2003 study and Yarhouse and colleagues' 2009 study.[8] "Ambient" harassing comments were "actions that take place within the environment but are not directed at a specific target, such as the telling of anti-LGB jokes that can be heard by anyone within earshot." "Personal" harassing comments, which were "directly targeted acts, such as being called 'dyke' to one's face."[9] Both intentional and unintentional nudity were found to be problematic, mostly among male students. However, a few female students also noted that there was intentional and unintentional immodesty on their dorm floors, which made them feel uncomfortable. LGB and SSA students and alumni also felt that their campuses seemed to heavily promote opposite-sex dating, which made them feel left out and uncomfortable.

Fifth, several respondents expressed feelings of anger and frustration from their experiences at Christian colleges and universities. These emotions were not just expressed by students and alumni who disagreed with the school. Even students who held to a TVS and agreed with the institutional policy on homosexuality expressed feelings of anger and frustration. At times, the venting of anger and frustration turned into rants, which may be typical of this age group. Some respondents used all capital letters and others expressed their anger through expletives. There could also have been a sense that the LGB and SSA students did not fully understand all other aspects of Christian higher education. A Christian college and university community consists of more than just students, but also people who are not on campus (e.g., trustees, donors, constituents, alumni, etc.). Although this research did not delve more deeply into attempting to ascertain the sources of their anger and frustration, listening to the anger and frustration of LGB and SSA students may prevent or lessen pent-up emotions.

Sixth, respondents did report positive support from students, staff, and faculty. Although many respondents expressed their fear of how others would respond, overwhelmingly respondents reported that their friends were very supportive after their disclosure. There were even some positive

8. Rankin, *Campus Climate*, 4; Yarhouse et al., "Listening to Sexual Minorities," 104.

9. Silverschanz et al., 180. See Appendix E for more discussion on the use of "personal" and "ambient" heterosexist harassment.

and supportive responses from friends who disagreed with the respective respondent's view of sexuality, yet still extended grace and compassion.

Conclusions Related to Recommendations

The research question also examined recommendations on how to make the campus climate at Christian colleges and universities less marginalizing for LGB and SSA students. There were four conclusions related to the recommendations of the respondents. First, Scripture suggests that a response to LGB and SSA students should begin with a posture of compassion. Administrators, staff, and faculty should strive to make their campuses less marginalizing for any student or for any group of students. The connection between loving one's neighbor and loving the stranger and sojourner "as yourself" in Leviticus 19:18 and 34 is a challenge to those working in Christian higher education to love the LGB and SSA students who feel marginalized.

Second, institutional policies must be clearer and applied consistently. As noted previously, a negative correlation was observed among respondents who indicated a level of agreement regarding the items about whether God blesses same-sex unions and whether they agree with the school's lifestyle statement. Those who believe that God blesses same-sex unions tended to disagree with the lifestyle statement and desired that language related to same-sex sexual practice be removed. Those who believe homosexuality is a sin tended to agree with the lifestyle statement and expressed an appreciation for the establishment of healthy boundaries. Wentz and Wessel also found that all eight of their respondents initially held to a TVS and chose their schools because of the institutional policy against same-sex sexual practice.[10] Although all of Wentz and Wessel's respondents later held to a PVS and disagreed with their school's position against same-sex sexual practice, the respondents from this research showed that there were some students who continue to support their schools' policies on sexual behavior. Among these respondents who held to a TVS, many did comment that institutional policies on homosexuality were easily misunderstood. It would be helpful for institutional policies to state that having same-sex attractions is not volitional and not considered outside of the lifestyle agreement. In addition, "homosexual behavior" should not be used since most respondents complained that it was vague. Alternative wording is suggested in the

10. Wentz and Wessel, 45.

following section. There should also be consistency regarding the manner in which other sexual sins are dealt with. Respondents perceived that heterosexual sex outside of marriage was dealt with less severely than same-sex sexual practice.

Third, efforts can be made to improve the campus climate for LGB and SSA students. Four ways to improve the climate of their campuses emerged from the data. One way was to raise awareness about sexuality and about LGB and SSA people through sensitivity training. This training can help improve the attitudes of other students and could possibly be scheduled during orientation at the beginning of each year. A second way to reduce hurtful and derogatory comments was by educating the students on which words to use and which words to avoid when talking about sexuality, as such education can help decrease hurtful and derogatory comments. In addition, staff, faculty, and resident directors should address such matters with students who make the hurtful and derogatory comments. Unfortunately, students often do not realize that their words are hurtful and say things out of ignorance. Therefore, confronting people who make hurtful and derogatory comments must be done graciously. A third way was to reduce intentional or unnecessary nudity and immodesty in the dorms. It is difficult to limit the unintentional nudity, such as male students taking showers. However, these students should respect others and should not joke around by rubbing their genitals on someone else or humping another person. A fourth way was that celibate singles should be honored and never made to feel "left out." This is very difficult on Christian college and university campuses that place a heavy emphasis on opposite-sex dating. Activities should be planned that do not have so much emphasis on "hooking up" and finding the right mate.

Fourth, respondents wanted their schools to form support groups for LGB and SSA students. They wanted a safe place for students who affirm the school's policy and desire assistance and accountability. There was also the recommendation to provide more mentoring opportunities for students by staff, faculty, or upperclassmen.

Action Steps: Clarity, Change, and Community

When taking action to reduce marginalization of LGB and SSA students, those working in Christian institutions of higher education must think of every student as *one of their own*. There is a responsibility for professionals working at Christian colleges and universities to care for all of their students. The goal is not only that students would gain an education, but also that students would grow and develop personally, relationally, emotionally, and spiritually. However, this development will be greatly hindered if a student feels marginalized. Just as Jesus had compassion for the marginalized populations of his culture, Christian professionals in higher education should have compassion for marginalized students. Just as Jesus saved the life of an adulteress and, without condemning her, said, "Go, and from now on sin no more" (John 8:11), those working in Christian colleges and universities should treat all students in a manner that is "full of grace and truth" (John 1:14). There is no question that balancing this tension between remaining both full of grace and full of truth is challenging and difficult. Contextualizing the gospel to everyday life requires extensive thought and effort, yet the gospel's deepest imperatives implore Christians to do so at any cost. God's common grace is withheld from no one, thus compassion for LGB and SSA students should not be withheld.

Below are action steps that have emerged from data in the previous chapters and from interactions that the researcher has had studying and teaching at Christian colleges and universities, as well as engaging with other professionals of Christian institutions of higher education. These action steps should not be viewed as exhaustive or conclusive. This is not a step-by-step formula guaranteed to solve the problem of marginalization and to make every LGB and SSA student feel safe and happy. Rather, these action steps should be viewed as the beginning of a process, as a springboard catalyzing a unified campus effort, and as the beginning of an intercollegiate effort between different colleges and universities. The answer will not be solved merely by student development professionals, residence life professionals, or by any other department acting in isolation. A concerted effort that produces movement toward success will only be realized when there is cooperation from every level, top to bottom. Therefore, the action steps below are for trustees, presidents, vice presidents, deans, directors, resident directors, faculty, staff, and anyone else involved at a Christian college or university. Battles are never won with a single soldier. Success requires working together.

In addition to a collaborative and integrated approach, action steps should focus not just on changing individuals without addressing the underlying impact of the campus culture. This neglect will result in futile efforts. Marginalization of LGB and SSA students at Christian institutions of higher education is influenced by the historical context of the school and the culture of the campus. Therefore, action steps must not only be a unified effort, but also must focus on transforming the campus culture as well. *Reducing marginalization of LGB and SSA students can be accomplished while holding fast to the traditional view of sexuality and without changing the institutional position on same-sex sexual practice.* There are thirty-four action steps, grouped into seven categories: (1) Clarity of institutional policies; (2) Culture change campuswide (3) Culture change classrooms; (4) Culture change dorms; (5) Culture change programming; (6) Community building; and (7) Campus beyond.

Clarity of institutional policies

1. Bring clarity to the institutional policy on homosexuality

The culture of colleges and universities is shaped by historical context, denominational affiliation, and institutional policies. Not much can be done to change the first two, but institutional polices can be added, clarified, and expanded. When outsiders ask about a school's response to homosexuality, the institutional policy will most likely be mentioned and, as a result, scrutinized. It was no surprise that respondents of this study with a PVS disagreed with their schools' institutional policies; however, even some participants with a TVS felt that the wording of the policies could have been better. Hence, there is a need for clarity. The policy must be grounded in and reference Scripture, the school's religious identity, possible denominational affiliation, and the core doctrinal statement. Begin with a clear articulation that sexual intimacy is reserved only for a husband and a wife in marriage. Provide a robust biblical and theological justification for marriage prior to explaining what the school does *not* allow.

Many institutional policies use the phrase "homosexual behavior," which is less ambiguous than "homosexuality," but university leaders cannot assume that students realize this terminology refers *only* to sexual intimacy. Vagueness leads to confusion, and a fearful and closeted freshman could easily misunderstand that "homosexual behavior" encompasses even the mere experience of same-sex attraction. Policies must distinguish between attraction and behavior, communicating that sexual activity is prohibited but not same-sex attractions. Although precision in the institutional policy wording is paramount, a long list of every prohibited act should be avoided at all costs. Rather, phraseology that is broad enough, but not too broad is preferred. The researcher suggests "same-sex sexual practice" over "homosexual behavior." This language is broader than the more precise, yet a bit inappropriate term "sexual intercourse," but it does not infer same-sex attractions. Sexual practice is also inclusive of erotic sexual activity leading up to intercourse, while differentiating it from healthy, intimate same-sex friendships that should be greatly encouraged at Christian colleges and universities.

Some more conservative schools may also want to preclude hand holding, hugging, or kissing. If an institution is concerned about these behaviors, "same-sex sexual practice and romantic relationships" may be used. This phrase would then distinguish between two same-sex partners holding hands and two best friends holding hands. The focus is then placed upon the intent of the action being exclusive, romantic intimacy as opposed to simply an intimate friendship. Students often argue that it is inconsistent to prohibit two people of the same sex to date while two people of the opposite sex can date as long as they are abstaining from sex. These two scenarios are not analogous. An opposite-sex romantic relationship between two unmarried people can culminate in a union that would be blessed by God, according to the TVS. However, a same-sex romantic relationship could not culminate in a union that would be blessed by God. A better analogy would be a married male student in a romantic relationship with another female student who is not his wife. If they are holding hands and studying together all the time on campus without having sex, this would still not be allowed and they would most likely require a meeting with the dean.

2. Communicate pastoral compassion in the institutional policy

This is one of the most important action steps. Many Christian colleges and universities have updated and expanded their policy statements in light of current events, such as the legalization of same-sex marriage. Although there may be legal pressure to tighten up the institutional stance on same-sex sexual practice, such measures can be desperately lacking in the area of pastoral compassion. These policies represent the institution's stance on homosexuality, and if these policies do not communicate any compassion for LGB and SSA students, then they communicate, albeit possibly inadvertently, that the institution does not have any compassion for LGB and SSA students. If these policies convey merely right and wrong—that is, only what to do and not do—then they may create a culture more akin to legalism than a gospel community of grace and truth. If these policies relay that ethics are the only concern, then administrators, faculty, and staff will have little pastoral guidance when ministering to LGB and SSA students. Policies should not just state what is right and wrong; they should also articulate the institution's desire to minister to the LGB and SSA student. Without pastoral compassion, policies will not communicate hope to the students. The institutional policy must not be read solely from a legal perspective, but also from the perspective of a fearful freshman who is not yet open about her or his sexuality. She or he may want help, but feels trapped. Remember, several respondents held to a TVS, agreed with the institutional policies against same-sex sexual practice, chose the school because of the institutional polices, and want the policies to stay the same. Not all LGB and SSA students are against the statement. But respondents do believe that the policies do not communicate compassion.

Several Christian colleges and universities have included a paragraph of pastoral compassion, which is good. But having it come after multiple pages of scriptural defense for biblical sexuality may cause such efforts to come across as disingenuous, insincere, or as mere afterthoughts. Biola University includes a thorough and well-written pastoral and compassionate statement. The section from the Biola University Student Handbook is provided below.

> Biola University believes that students are best supported if they are able to share their questions, struggles, or their self-understanding with trusted others, including those in Student Development. Concerns about sexuality may be difficult to disclose, but struggling in silence is a far greater challenge. In all such personal issues, Student Development staff members are committed to discretion, sensitivity, confidentiality, compassion, and redemption.
>
> When a student approaches us and communicates that he or she is struggling with same-sex behavior, same-sex attraction and/or sexual orientation issues we aim to offer safety that promotes openness. We pledge to extend compassion and care communicating personal acceptance, while providing accountability and assistance supporting students in their desire to live consistently with Christian teaching.
>
> In regards to behavior, all students are responsible for their actions, sexual and otherwise. At Biola, we are committed to helping our students develop toward Christ-like maturity in their daily practices. With this said, sexual behavior contrary to Biola's

community standards will be addressed through a disciplinary process. As noted earlier, in all disciplinary matters we will seek to be redemptive and developmental in the lives of the individuals involved.

We do lament the insensitive and often callous treatment that students working through these issues may have received from the Christian community. All members of the Biola Community are expected to treat one another with respect and Christ-like compassion. Insults, slurs and other forms of derogatory speech have no place in a Christian community. Through faculty & staff training, peer education and example we seek to educate staff and students about the harm caused by disrespectful or flippant speech around this topic.

Due to the complexity of issues related to same-sex behavior, same-sex attraction and sexual orientation, we are committed to engaging this conversation with courage, humility, prayerfulness and care. We believe, in accordance with Scripture, that we are all broken. Therefore, a primary goal of Student Development at Biola is to help each student find God in the midst of their unique history and struggles and discern how to walk with Him and others along the way.[11]

These five paragraphs communicating a robust, pastoral, and compassionate response complement well with the statements prohibiting "homosexual behavior" and "homosexual conduct." Thus they communicate both grace *and* truth in the institutional policy, as opposed to a truth-only document devoid of grace or hope for the one struggling with same-sex desires. There are two noteworthy aspects of the above pastoral statement. First, it encourages students to share with trusted others and not struggle in silence. The researcher also suggests to add a statement such as, "We believe the best place to be navigating through issues of sexual identity is in Christian community."

Second, the above statement mentions the harm of derogatory speech. Clearly and publicly denouncing hurtful comments against LGB and SSA people sends a strong message that the school cares for all students. The researcher would suggest adding in the last sentence of the third paragraph "restorative" so that it would read, "in all disciplinary matters we will seek to be redemptive, restorative, and developmental in the lives of the individuals involved." Discipline should be restorative in nature (2 Cor 2:5–11;

11. Biola University, *Undergraduate Student Handbook.*

Matt 18:15–17; Gal 6:1; Jas 5:19–20), and even in situations of dismissal, there can be a path toward the student returning to campus.

3. Apply policies consistently

Several respondents of this study perceived that the institutional polices were applied inconsistently, with same-sex sexual practices being subjected to harsher discipline. Heterosexual sex outside of marriage should not be treated differently than homosexual sex. Many factors influence the disciplinary process, including a student's forthrightness, humility, sense of remorse, and repentance. Certainly, discipline should be decided case by case; however, heterosexual sex outside of marriage should not be treated less severely than homosexual sex. From an outsider's perspective, inconsistency may appear to be present when in reality it is not. Unfortunately, in most situations, the student facing discipline feels that the process is unfair. The reality is that the dean of students is obligated to keep the disciplinary process confidential, and the spread of the news around campus about the unfair discipline is often one-sided. Not much can be changed to keep such instances from occurring. With that being said, a discipline committee can have an annual internal assessment to review the committee's decisions and the consistency of those decisions in light of previous situations. The dean must be intentional about building relationships with student leaders wherein trust, integrity, compassion, and consistency can be relayed. The researcher believes that general positive or negative attitudes toward the dean over how she or he handles disciplinary cases often have a direct correlation to the depth and quality of relationships the dean has with students. Therefore, having a firm but personal dean can help in this area. The student development and residence life staff should also help communicate to student leaders and students about the purpose of discipline to be restorative and not simply punitive.

4. Pastoral clarity in the admissions application

LGB and SSA students are usually exposed to the institutional policy on homosexuality long before they step foot on campus. Most admissions applications for Christian colleges and universities mention the lifestyle agreement and require assent from applicants to follow those standards. A few respondents of this study chose to attend their school specifically because of the institutional policy prohibiting homosexual practice in the hopes that their attractions would go away. However, many students felt the policies were unclear and left no room for strugglers. Pastoral compassion in the institutional policies is often lacking in the admissions application as well. Although applicants must agree to abide by the lifestyle agreement, the researcher suggests that the application state that the school desires to journey, grow, and mature together through these important and formative years of young adulthood. Students are not expected to be perfect or never to be tempted with sin.

Admissions applications often are updated annually, and students, faculty, and staff should be invited to provide constructive criticism when changes are made. An informal group of volunteer advisors who are not in the admissions department can be gathered to help review and assess the language in light of evolving cultural trends. When assessing the application, ask questions such as: Does the application communicate the school's ethos? Does the portion regarding consent to the lifestyle agreement possess a compassionate tone? If the admissions application is the first exposure to the policy against same-sex sexual practice, does it provide hope for the struggler? Does the language and tone lead to a sense that attending this school will be a redemptive place to pursue holiness? First impressions have a tendency to last, and schools should put much effort into putting forth the best and most clear message in their admissions applications.

5. Survey students

Although a survey made available to the whole student body would be overwhelming, surveying student leaders regarding institutional policies can be more manageable. Are the policies clear? Do the policies communicate compassion? Would a struggler reading the policies feel like hiding or seeking help? Is there anything that needs to be added? Is there anything that should be taken out?

Culture change campuswide

6. Sensitivity training

Student development and residence life professionals are often the ones planning sensitivity training and sessions to increase cultural competency with a focus on the students. However, changing the campus culture cannot focus only on the students. It must be at all levels, even at the top. *Therefore, there must be sensitivity training on homosexuality for every trustee board.* Changes in culture happen so fast and the understanding of sexuality has arguably changed more than anything else. This often leaves the older generation disconnected from the younger generation. Students almost speak another language when it comes to sexuality, and things that might seem foreign and even disgusting for older adults may not be considered abnormal for students. Today's media and culture is saturated with messages encouraging behavior that is contrary to a gospel-centered life..

The researcher believes that campus culture change cannot occur without the trustees being also involved with this transformation. The trustee board is responsible for the stewardship and good governance of the institution. It is also responsible to ensure that the institution remains true to its mission and theological foundation. Therefore, when it comes to the topic of homosexuality, the board may fully understand biblical truth that same-sex sexual practice is sinful; however, the board may miss the redemptive grace aspect. Trustees may be aware of the vocal gay activist alumni, but not realize that there are struggling, closeted students who hold to the TVS, yet are too afraid to open up to others about their sexuality. Trustee boards must receive training not just on homosexuality, but be made aware of the current issues on their campuses regarding LGB and SSA students.

Campus-wide sensitivity training should also include administration, staff, faculty, and students. Segments of campus professionals often neglected when it comes to training on homosexuality are non-student development and non-residence life staff, such as the director of international students, coaches, career development staff, health center staff, director of student programs, ministry department staff, multicultural development staff, chaplaincy staff, etc. These are all staff members who have great influence and deep impact in the lives of students outside the classroom. These staff members mentor, advise, coach, and do one-on-one life with students. They are doing life with the students and are hands-on in their identity formation. And yet, there is a significant absence of training for non-student development and non-residence life staff who have clear connections and relationships with students. Coaches spend hours each day in practice and travel extensively with their players for games. Sick students in their most vulnerable moments often open up to health center nurses regarding their sexuality. A minority student already feeling out of place may find safety in the multicultural development office and come out of the closet to the director. And yet, more often than not, these staff members feel ill equipped to engage and minister to these students. Sensitivity training must include all campus professionals who develop any type of meaningful relationship with students.

7. Create an assessment tool

Before changing the campus climate, the school will need to know the state of the campus. What is the climate? The Intercultural Development Inventory (IDI) is an assessment tool on the issue of racism. There is no similar tool for sexual identity, and if one were developed similar to IDI, it would probably not align with the values and theological convictions of Christian colleges and universities. However, a school could develop something similar and more simplistic. This will help determine those areas where improvement is necessary.

8. Develop a glossary of terms

As previously stated, the terminology and nomenclature related to issues of sexuality are rapidly changing. Commonly used language from as recently as five years ago, and certainly twenty years ago (when the researcher identified as a gay man), went out of use and differ from what is spoken today. Unless a person is actively working in a field related to sexuality, it would be nearly impossible to stay abreast of all the new vocabulary related to sexual identity used by this younger generation. Students, however, because of their heightened exposure to media, street talk, and interaction with friends who identify as LGB or SSA, quickly recognize and adopt the latest terms and slang. If individuals within the college and university leadership expect to be heard and establish communication with the students on their campuses, they must be able to stay abreast of the words and definitions that are evolving into modern parlance. Even the use of "lesbian," "gay," or "bisexual" by an individual is sometimes equated with same-sex sexual practice or with a PVS. However, this research has shown that some students identify as LGB but have a TVS and are called to a life of celibacy. For reasons like this, an in-house glossary of terms would be immensely helpful for administrators, faculty, and staff. This glossary would be more like a living document, one that is regularly reviewed, amended, and updated.

The glossary provided at the beginning of this book should prove useful in helping school leadership establish an initial baseline, which can be made available in-house as it continues to evolve over time.

9. Develop a resource page

Faculty and staff often feel ill-equipped when approached by a student who opens up about his or her sexuality. One way of providing them a level of readiness and confidence in these situations would be the availability of an in-house resource page for faculty and staff. This resource page could include suggested books and websites deemed useful and biblically grounded, as well as a list of people on campus who may be better equipped, trained, and/or experienced to minister and walk with LGB and SSA students. Furthermore, the resources listed should be customized for the specific institution, bearing in mind theological traditions and denominational affiliations. Yet even with these types of references to recommend, the goal of this document is not to suggest that the faculty and staff pass the student off to someone else. It is not designed as a university-sanctioned excuse for being dismissive of an LGB or SSA student at a moment of high vulnerability, thereby communicating that these are matters ought to be brought to someone else.

The fact that a student might dare approach a professor or other staff member is likely because a level of great trust and personal relationship exists between the two—a scenario that yields precisely the kind of ingredients that can lead to a compassionate, pastoral handling of the situation. The resource page should include ideas for continuing support, including qualified individuals who can lend their expertise concerning a variety of disciplines and issues. Although for some, there is a sense of inadequacy when it comes to the topic of sexual identity. Every faculty and staff member is equipped to help. Being an expert on homosexuality is not required to be a friend, to listen, to have compassion, and to simply walk with an LGB or SSA student. Being a friend is often better than giving the impression that one has all the answers. Additional practical tips can be provided, such as staying calm, thanking the person for sharing, being a good listener, asking open-ended questions, and most importantly, inquiring how the student's faith plays into this whole process.

10. Form a committee

Form a committee on sexual identity to keep abreast of current issues regarding homosexuality. Schools already have many committees; however, not having a comprehensive and ongoing redemptive response to homosexuality and LGB and SSA students can have greater implications. The researcher believes that the importance of this is so great that the committee's genesis should come from the president to function as his advisory council. A single person is unable to be aware of all the dimensions of this issue, while a group of select people can much more effectively assist the administration in monitoring events, trends, and attitudes concerning sexual identity in the culture, in the church, and on the campus. Each college and university has unique aspects of its makeup and constituency, including denominational ties, theological background, student body makeup, regional culture, Christian and non-Christian ratio, and majors represented (nursing school, film school, music school, business school, education, social work, etc.). The committee should work closely with public relations and alumni relations because of the strong influence of the institution's wider constituency. Therefore, the makeup of this committee should include representatives from many facets of the school's broader community. Below is a sample list of advisory council members combined from a few institutions that have an existing committee.

1. President
2. Provost
3. Chaplain
4. Executive assistant to the president
5. Dean of students
6. Directors of media relations, alumni relations, human resources, counseling center, career services, admissions, residence life, and student health services
7. Professors from the Bible/theology department, communications department, and fine arts department
8. Students; president of student government and student chaplain
9. Alumnus/alumna

The purposes of the committee should suit the needs of each college or university. Some are involved with programming and scheduling events on sexuality, while others are not involved. Some have decided that the committee would not speak to the institution or for the institution, but would simply advise the administration. Some have been a part of rewriting the institutional policy on same-sex sexual practice, while others only provided suggestions. The frequency of meetings can be twice a semester. The following is the purpose statement of a committee on sexual identity from an institution as a sample.

> Advises the administration on campus awareness and response to the topic of sexual identity affecting the college/university and the church. Provides support for campus leaders in dealing with issues of human sexuality drawn from the culture, the church and the campus.

11. Denounce derogatory comments and actions

Whenever an incident of a derogatory comment or action occurs that brings the school into public awareness or simply becomes widely known on campus, do not be afraid to give a strong public denouncement. When the aforementioned events of racism at the University of Missouri's campus were first reported, students felt that there was a lack of clear denunciation by the school and president, which created the impression that these issues were irrelevant or trivial to the school. Christian colleges and universities must be intentional about not giving the impression of being apathetic when students are intentionally treated in a derogatory way. With wisdom and discernment, make a concise but strong statement in a venue where most of the student body would be present, such as at chapel.

One example that took place on a Christian campus involved an unknown person or group of persons who used baby powder to write the word "fags" on a particular dorm floor where several students were known or suspected to be openly gay or struggling. As news of the event spread across campus, the school seized the opportunity in their regular chapel service to denounce these harassing actions, clearly communicating to the student body that such behavior did not represent the Christian values of the school and would not be tolerated. The school was able to communicate that holding to the TVS does not mean that it is permissible to demean students who experience attractions toward the same sex. Negative situations such as this can provide positive opportunities to provide a tangible example to the students of balancing grace and truth. The institution can strongly defend those who may be mistreated and communicate that those actions do not represent the school.

12. Celebrate singleness and do not idolize marriage

One of the most unaddressed issues at every Christian college or university is the overemphasis on and almost idolization of courtship, dating, and marriage while simultaneously disparaging singleness. This culture has probably been a core part of any Christian campus from the outset of the school. This overemphasis can create a persistent source of discomfort for LGB and SSA students who have chosen not to pursue same-sex romantic relationships. By no standard of Scripture do young men and women who are married represent the highest ideal and goal for all believers. Certainly, the covenant relationship of marriage instituted by God is very good. And certainly, opposite-sex romantic and sexually pure relationships heading toward marriage should be applauded and encouraged. But it is not the only example for human flourishing. This lifts up one good thing at the expense of the equally good status of singleness. Sometimes, good things can turn into idols (e.g., jobs, children, recreation, etc.), and for many Christians the overemphasis on marriage comes perilously close to idolatry of a good thing.

Some of the most cherished traditions of a Christian college or university include engagement rituals between university coeds. But when the standard script of the admissions tour for prospective students intentionally mentions—while *coincidentally* passing the bell tower—the ritual for newly engaged couples, it is clear that the overemphasis begins even before students move onto campus. The unintended consequence is that those who do not pair off are the unlucky ones and miss out on this beloved tradition and much, much more. Christian colleges and universities must be careful to celebrate both the goodness of marriage and the goodness of singleness. With the abundant attention and priority on courtship, dating, and marriage, there must be an intentional effort to value those who are not in a relationship, whether it is a dorm floor activity or an all-school event. Chapel messages should include messages on singleness that move beyond the abstinence-before-marriage talk or how-to-make-yourself-ready-for-your-future-spouse message. If the TVS means that LGB and SSA students must not act on their desires, then for them the reality is being single for a period in their lives if not their entire lives. Yet right now, Christian singles do not have a healthy context to thrive on a Christian campus. Without reclaiming a robust biblical and practical theology of singleness,[12] Christian colleges and universities may not even be ready to tackle the issue of sexual identity.

Culture change classrooms

13. Insert sexuality into curriculum

Most schools have a course on sexuality and some have a course specifically on sexual identity (or at least in part). However, only a small segment of the student body population can benefit per semester because of the limited class size or prerequisite requirement for psychology/counseling majors only. There must be a more comprehensive approach, one that seeks to contextualize the subject among other fields of study, helping students grapple with how one's viewpoints on sexuality impact Christian thinking on theology, biology, philosophy, history, business, arts, communication, and other disciplines. Engage department heads and communicate to them the importance of incorporating LGB and SSA issues into the classroom. Once they realize the significance, they will be able to persuade (without enforcing) colleagues to creatively and thoughtfully insert the topic of sexual identity into their lectures. In addition, it is imperative that professors present the information in a redemptive and grace-filled way that exemplifies grace and truth. Professors can mention LGB artists or writers as an example of God's common grace and do this without disdain or ridicule. Some of the greatest musicians and authors (e.g., Mozart and Hemingway) lived in ways that did not align with Christian living, and yet rarely are they spoken of with disdain or ridicule among Christians. Taken as a whole, these threads of awareness and openness taking place in many different classrooms across campus, happening in such highly intentional and thoughtful ways, will have a positive effect on the campus climate encouraging strugglers that they don't need to hide and allow trusted Christian friends to journey with them.

12. Barry Danylak has written the best resource on a biblical theology of singleness, *A Biblical Theology of Singleness*. It is must read. It is 28 pages but rich. It can only be purchased from the UK, but they can ship internationally. Here is the link, www.grovebooks. co.uk/products/b-45-a-biblical-theology-of-singleness.

14. Hiring of faculty and staff

With the increasing need to be aware of issues related to sexuality, administration should look to hire faculty who possess a special cultural competency and sensitivity in the area of sexual identity. Although this cultural competency would most likely not be communicated in a résumé, injecting an open-ended question into the standard interview process may reveal an individual who is competent to care for and minister to the LGB and SSA student. The institution should also be open to hiring an SSA faculty member. This possibility may not have ever been considered, but it should. Most likely, many campuses already have faculty who are SSA but are afraid to disclose. This study has focused solely upon students; however, there are undoubtedly faculty members who are struggling alone. Not every faculty member needs to be open, but having a select few know can become a valuable benefit to the institution. These individuals can be a very helpful resource as they bring their own personal experience and help their schools understand LGB and SSA students.

15. Interdepartmental partnerships

Usually, it is student development and residence life staff receiving training related to LGB and SSA students, and not faculty. Yet professors are the ones who are more likely to be approached their students, than student development or residence life staff. Professors are face-to-face with students every day and may be viewed as friends, and not the police or disciplinary dean. With or without training or preparation, faculty members are sometimes the ones on the front lines at critical moments in students' lives. This observable dynamic calls for increased partnership between faculty and student development and residence life staff. Although faculty-wide training can be beneficial, this takes much convincing and planning. Instead, student development and residence life staff can easily ascertain from students who are the handful of more approachable professors that students trust. Meet these faculty members in their offices and communicate with them the shared desire to minister well to LGB and SSA students. Offer to share information, to provide training resources, and to be a confidential sounding board. Because professors are often so busy with their course load and with grading papers, be sure to follow through with an email, phone call, or even lunch in the cafeteria.

16. Student course evaluations

At the end of every semester, students are invited to fill out a survey evaluating the pedagogy of the professor and whether course objectives were met. Regrettably, little regard is actually given to these evaluations, largely because of the unreliability of the data. Many are dutifully checked off by students, merely to complete the exercise in as little time as possible; others are heaped with nice but unnecessary praise; others are influenced by poor test grades and other factors that skew the reporting. Although the efficacy of these evaluations continues to be contested, the elimination of course evaluations will most likely not occur any time soon. In spite of this, student evaluations can be a helpful gauge for the climate in the classroom.

One of the key distinctions that separate Christian colleges from their secular counterparts is the expectation that professors are more involved in the lives of their students, not merely in their scholastic endeavors. Therefore, the introduction of a question into the course evaluation process could serve as both an accountability factor as well as a helpful diagnostic tool. "Do you feel comfortable or safe to open up with this professor about a personal matter?" A question like this could also communicate to the students that the administration expects professors to demonstrate and embody these principles.

Culture change dorms

17. Careful selection of residence life director

Changing the culture in the dorms is not easy and it involves a concerted effort between students and staff. But there is one staff position in particular who has a comparatively larger impact on dorm culture: the residence life director. The residence life director selects and influences the resident directors. The resident directors select and influence the resident assistants. The resident assistants influence the students on their floor. A director who unequivocally agrees with the institutional policy against same-sex sexual practice, but sees no need to minister to a SSA student, can create a climate on campus that pushes strugglers deeper into secrecy. And yet a director who is very compassionate, but believes that the school should not make such a big deal about homosexuality and should be united with a diversity of opinions on same-sex relationships, can create a campus climate that has a tendency to push against the administration to change their policies.

The researcher visited a particular Christian college. It was highly conservative, holding officially and unwaveringly to a TVS, yet the campus had become quite progressive in its tone, tenor, and makeup. This contrast between stated policy and prevailing opinion had begun to create a clash between student body and administration. The director of residence life, obviously aware of these tensions, and whose role and influence is highly involved in navigating the everyday waters between such competing viewpoints, has taken a position of riding the fence rather than supporting the university's position statement with truth *and* grace. This has proved problematic in a number of ways, creating a vacuum of clear leadership in which confusion and conflict have only increased. The director of residence life is in a key position to help maintain clarity and consistency regarding the school's policies on same-sex sexual practice and the school's desire to be pastoral and compassionate. The resident director possesses an important role in how such policies and virtues are lived out, upheld, and communicated on campus. Christian colleges need the right people in these roles, ones who can nimbly walk the twin virtues of grace and truth on issues that are potentially divisive as those involving sexual identity.

18. Hiring resident directors and resident assistants

Just as careful selection is necessary for the top leadership role in the office of residence life, so must be the hiring of individual residence hall directors and their staff of resident assistants (RAs). The interview process should include a question related to LGB and SSA students. "If I was a student on your floor and came out to you, what would you do or say?" "What would you do if a student in your dorm was in a same-sex relationship?" "What would you do if a student continuously tells gay jokes and calls people 'fags'?" The times call for brave, compassionate, well-reasoned, and responsible answers to questions such as these, and they should be asked of residence life staff long before situations arise where they must deal with them in real time.

19. Resident assistant training

Few places in life pose more of a challenge to personal space and sensitivities than the college residence hall. The mingling of personalities, lifestyles, and viewpoints, shared within such close proximity with one another, creates a continual mixture of potential irritations and insecurities. For LGB and SSA students, the hazards and struggles can be even greater. The role of the resident assistant (RA) is extremely valuable in determining whether this dangerous mix can be harmful or transformative for students. RA training is an important, ongoing process that must include training on matters related to sexuality broadly and homosexuality specifically. These student leaders should be empowered to confidently manage situations with truth and grace. Confrontation is usually the biggest hurdle to overcome for resident assistants. There should be many training sessions on how an RA can confront well. RAs should also be coached on how to confront students who consistently make gay jokes and derogatory remarks about homosexuality. Although the resident assistants cannot be constantly patrolling, they should not initiate or encourage nudity in floor games or jokes. And when things get out of hand, the student leader should be prepared to settle things back down. The RAs should all study the glossary of terms made available to faculty and staff. One effective method of training is mock scenarios when RAs pair up and address any number of potential situations. Afterward, they should regroup to discuss and debrief on what went well and what could have been improved.

20. More privacy in men's bathrooms

One of the most challenging parts of residence life for LGB and SSA students is the inevitable interactions that occur in the bathroom, and Christian colleges seeking to be sensitive to these concerns should address them with proactive measures. Among the more bewildering realities of residence life is the widespread discrepancy of privacy considerations that exist between male and female bathroom facilities. Women's dorms are designed to respect the privacy of their female students. However, men's dorms do not reflect this same consideration As much as there is concern for women to have privacy in their showering area, there should also be consideration for men's privacy. Those who are responsible for creating and rethinking how these spaces are constructed should give attention to the men's bathrooms and showers in their residence halls.

Some of these changes would be more or less difficult than others. Retrofitting existing residence halls to create more privacy in the showers may be a big investment; however with some creativity, a less expensive way can be discovered to accomplish the same effect. Two sets of shower curtains with stall walls in between can create privacy when showering and changing. All urinals in men's bathrooms should have barriers in between them—not only in the dorms, but also in the bathrooms of academic buildings and athletic building looker rooms. These two examples would not be too costly, but it would bring the structures of the school in line with the school's ethos of respect for every individual. And as a possible incentive, creating more privacy in the bathroom may make the campus more appealing for outside groups to come in during the summer, thus bringing in extra revenue. Especially in the design phase of new residence centers, most Christian colleges and universities are following the example of others who are moving away from community bathrooms and communal showers, opting instead for private bathroom facilities that respect the individual's privacy.

Physical structures, of course, will not change people's hearts. The most important areas of emphasis in regard to sexuality should be the changing of campus culture to reflect Christian thinking and compassionate understanding. But if the culture is changing while the physical structures do not reflect the same ethos, the speed of healthy change can be somewhat restricted by the lack of conformity with structures. The administrative decision to introduce such rudimentary changes as shower curtains in the showering areas, barriers between urinals, and other similar improvements communicates a larger message to residents that the university does care about these things. For in many respects, physical structures do influence culture. Change the bathroom, and you noticeably change the dynamics within the dorm. Architects intentionally design lounge areas to create an atmosphere of intimacy, fellowship, and community. Interior designers select styles and color palettes to produce a certain desired mood and ethos. Although the old-school norms of spartan living conditions seem inconsequential to some in leadership—perhaps even a manly rite of passage in toughening up for the world ahead—the reality is that *bathrooms often create a lot of anxiety and even shame, which is experienced on a daily basis for the four years a student lives on campus.* Christian schools that fail to address this often unspoken fear and shame are not treating their students with the respect that communicates understanding and compassion.

21. *Compassionate Discipline*

Disciplinary situations are typically unpleasant for everyone involved, but deans and residence life staff should resist the temptation to resolve the issue and hand down judgment too quickly. These difficult situations should be viewed as opportunities for relationship. Build compassion into the experience. If trust is built and the student opens up, there are often other underlying issues shared that are more pertinent than what brought the student in to begin with. Although the student may want to know what the consequence is, allow for time to consider all aspects of the situation and work for deeper change within a student's life. The life and future of a student is worth handling with patience, compassion, and wisdom. The ultimate goal of biblical discipline in the church is not simply the expulsion of sinners from fellowship, but rather the restoration of individuals' relationships with God and their fellow sisters and brothers. The goal of discipline on the Christian college campus should reflect this heightened desire for redemption as well. Discipline should be a potential pathway for bringing students back into alignment with what is best for both themselves and the healthy rhythms of the university.

Culture change programming

22. *Chapels and special events*

On most Christian campuses, regular chapel gatherings are the one place in which the entire student body comes together. As such, a very effective way to influence culture change on campus would be to utilize chapel programming to engage the student body on matters involving sexuality. When Millennials are asked what is the main issue of their generation, they always mention homosexuality. Unfortunately, students on Christian colleges and universities often graduate ill equipped to engage the culture on issues related to the gay community and SSA individuals. Addressing this relevant issue once a year in chapel is barely enough to prepare Christian students soon entering into a culture with a very different perspective on sexuality. And yet, having an expert on sexuality come to campus to do nothing but speak in chapel would not be the best use of her or his time, and it would be a missed opportunity for other teaching and training possibilities for students, staff, and faculty. With so much invested to bring a chapel speaker on campus, Christian colleges and universities must steward that time and those resources well.

Organize a special evening session after the chapel when the speaker can expand and provide more practical advice, including a question-and-answer time for the students. Allow time for training with student development and residence life staff. Coordinate sessions with student leaders and resident assistants. Inform the faculty and utilize the time that the speaker is on campus to provide some training as a faculty development session. If the speaker consents, arrange time to meet students individually or in groups. Consider expanding the visit to two days or even three days. Some schools will even incorporate the speaker in a chapel series that could also include evening sessions. A thirty-minute chapel message on sexuality once a year is hardly enough to equip students who are being inundated with messages about sexuality from culture and media. Let our Christian colleges and universities be institutions that train, equip, and prepare this younger generation to engage our culture well on this very relevant issue.

23. Listening sessions

Data gathered by the researcher confirmed that LGB and SSA students do not feel they have a voice that is heard. One respondent expressed how even the mere action of putting his thoughts down in the survey was healing for him. Other respondents also communicated a sense of woundedness, anger, frustration, and bitterness. This is only compounded when there is no outlet. Therefore, Christian colleges and universities can allow students to organize listening session events where students share about their own personal journey of living as an LGB or SSA person. LGB and SSA students can express their turmoil and their difficult experiences with other students. Listening to stories can be healing and helpful for everyone involved. It can be eye opening for listeners to get inside the thoughts of LGB and SSA students. It can be an opportunity for LGB and SSA students to diminish some of the frustration that actively breeds within the context of secrecy, silence, and feeling as if one has no voice. These sessions can be either dormwide or campuswide, but to respect the personal and private stories of students, they should not be intended to be open to the public. The listening session should be more along the lines of family discussions around the den or kitchen table, shared between people who care about one another and are seeking the best for everyone. They are safe places of gathering, which foster an atmosphere for people to be real and authentic. As such, what is shared would not be representative of the school's position, but rather reflect the experiences of students. This should be communicated to the students prior to and at the meeting.

24. Conversations around race, gender, and sexuality

The culture has been engaging in conversations around race, gender, and sexuality for years. In his 2013 inaugural speech, President Obama even made a connection between women's rights, civil rights, and gay rights. This connection seems to have become a standard comparison to the extent that many understand the fight for gay rights to be equivalent to or an extension of the fight for women's rights and civil rights. Unfortunately, in Christian circles this conversation is absent, and although there have been improvements in engaging on issues of race and gender, Christian colleges and universities need to start this broader conversation involving all three. This does not mean that the institution needs to agree with the comparison, but a healthy conversation would be to critically and biblically engage this assumption. Help students to understand the similarities and differences between race, gender, and sexuality. Initiate deeper dialogue regarding identity and how race, gender, and sexuality have been incorporated well or poorly. Why would race and gender be an aspect of one's identity? And why would sexuality and one's experience of attractions or desires for relationship possibly be a poor way to define oneself?

Community building

25. Support groups

Although this study revealed that respondents wanted their schools to have some form of a support group, there was nothing from the data providing details of what a support group would look like. Therefore, further research would need to be accomplished on support groups for LGB and SSA students at Christian colleges and universities. Should a group be student-run or staff-run? Should the emphasis be discipleship or social activities? Would it consist of students who hold to both a TVS and a PVS, or have separate groups? Some Christian colleges and universities already have support groups for LGB and SSA students. One issue that has arisen for groups that are more student-run is that there is a tendency to morph into an advocacy group that generally does not support a TVS and has a tone of challenging the school's stance on same-sex sexual practice. At one school where this occurred, an underground group for LGB and SSA students who held to a TVS formed as an alternative because they did not feel that the school-sanctioned group was a healthy or safe place for them. The difficulty of having a student-run group with students holding to both a TVS and a PVS is that there will be conflicting needs. One group of students is seeking support to help them to pursue celibacy and chastity, while the other group is seeking support to embrace and affirm same-sex romantic relationships. What seems to work best is to have a support group that is more staff led with a discipleship and mentoring focus.

26. Provide mentoring opportunities

Starting a support group takes much planning and foresight. The end goal may be unclear and the long-term benefits may be few. It does seem that support groups with a mentoring or discipleship focus are more ideal. However, mentoring and discipleship were really meant for one-on-one, and students can benefit greatly with one-on-one discipleship that is more personal and intimate. The unfortunately reality is that the process of re-cruiting available, capable, and godly mentors is always a difficult one. There are more students who want a mentor than there are mentors. Faculty and staff who may have the heart to be a mentor may not have the time for it, and those who become mentors may become overwhelmed by workload or coursework. One answer would be to contact off-campus constituents as potential mentors, such as local alumni, supporters, pastors, and ministry staff members. In addition, upperclass students may be willing to mentor younger freshmen.

The beauty of these relationships is that they transcend the one-note discussions surrounding any issues of same-sex attraction or similar strug-gles. The mentoring possibilities that a Christian college should want to provide are opportunities for students to grow in all aspects of their sanc-tification, being discipled and prayed for by an older, wiser believer with whom they can study the Bible and seek greater intimacy in their walk with Christ and their involvement in mission. Mentors would need to know they could be asked anything, and that they are not required to have the answer for every question. But primarily they provide a two-way street of blessing and spiritual renewal that is beneficial to any student desiring to grow in their faith.

27. Anonymous online support

This research confirmed that many LGB and SSA students are not yet ready to be open about their sexuality. A support group or mentor would benefit only students who are ready to be open. But what about those students who would not go to a group or share with their mentor about their experience of same-sex attractions? Can there be a way to provide support for students while allowing them some anonymity? For this reason, the researcher suggests the possibility of an online anonymous group where students can dialogue with staff or a counselor. This could possibly be a way to let these students know that they really are not alone and that there are people on campus willing to walk with them through this journey. Struggling alone is a context that breeds anxiety, fear, depression, and possibly even suicidality. Christian colleges and universities should not ignore and have more concern for silent strugglers. Anonymous online support may help bridge these students to staff who can help.

28. Healthy relationships vs. codependency

Christian colleges and universities do well to emphasize and encourage strong community and intimate friendships among fellow classmates. This emphasis makes Christian campuses stand out above other non-Christian campuses. Tight friendships, open fellowship, and trusting reliance on one another are hallmarks of a thriving Christian campus. However, what often gets overlooked is when a friendship becomes *too* dependent and turns into a "relationship addiction."[13] This is codependency, which is an unhealthy and dysfunctional reliance upon another. Even sound, healthy relationships can descend into codependency if the people involved are unaware and are not mindful of the types of boundaries needed to keep relationships healthy. Anyone can struggle with falling into codependent relationships, and for LGB and SSA students, the struggle is not just resisting same-sex attractions but also fleeing codependent tendencies. Sexual attractions are not the only issue to keep in mind.

13. Mental Health America, "Co-Dependency."

Codependency is relational idolatry, wherein a person elevates her or his need for someone else and validation is required in order for the person to feel valued and accepted. During college years, where young adults are constantly forming new connections and seeking to succeed socially, a caring campus will want to do everything possible to help them learn relational skills that will benefit them throughout life. But little guidance is offered to help them build and maintain healthy relationships that honor God. Residence life and student development staff can plan programming in which the characteristics of healthy relationships are presented to pursue and the characteristics of a codependent relationship are presented to avoid. Among the action steps needed for making any of these other action steps maximally beneficial is a purposeful aim at helping students learn how to interact with one another without being demanding of each other while building relationships that honor God.

29. Budget for more counselors

The counseling center should be a safe place where students can open up and know that the counselors are bound to confidentiality. Counselors are trained to listen and help clients process their own thoughts. Simply listening and lovingly speaking biblical truth is often better than having all the answers. The campus counseling staff may be the only line of help that the person feels comfortable approaching. Unfortunately, many schools have a waiting list for students to see a counselor. This should not be. Seek to increase the budget for more counselors. Another option would be utilizing interns from a local Christian graduate psychology or biblical counseling school. This would be a win-win situation for everyone. See if your school has a waiting list for the counseling center and if so, find ways to solve that problem.

30. Prayer groups

Not all schools are at a point where they are ready to form a support group for LGB and SSA students on campus. Support groups require a lot of careful planning and hard work to implement. However, starting a prayer group for students who personally experience same-sex attractions and for students who have loved ones in the gay community would not be too difficult. Groups can meet once a week or once a month without much of an agenda other than praying together. Praying with and for others breaks down walls and binds people together. What students usually want more is a safe community. A prayer group could provide that. The presence of a prayer group on campus could do much to enhance a true softening of hearts at the school and in the culture.

31. Interdepartmental focus prayer group

Usually only a handful of staff are actively engaging this issue and/or working with students navigating issues of sexual identity. The potential weight from what dealing with these matters can amass is often more than they can carry alone. Recognizing this difficulty and pressure, these staff members should take the initiative to meet regularly for prayer and support. Many of the requests that might arise within such pockets of prayer would need to stay anonymous and unspecified, but the unity created by praying together would still be a specific source of help and encouragement. Beyond prayer alone, groups like these could become places where ideas are shared, where advice is sought, and where collaboration can be fostered among those who are specifically tied to working with LGB and SSA students on campus.

Campus beyond

32. Intercollegiate focus group on sexual identity

All Christian colleges and universities are wrestling with issues of sexuality and should seek ways to improve in their care for LGB and SSA students. Some have had more experience than other schools. Some have come up with great ideas to work with their LGB and SSA students. Some have learned ways to educate their very conservative constituency. Some have developed wisdom from working through a difficult experience, maybe even something that had hit national media. With all these diverse, valuable experiences on campuses across the country, the need for each individual school to reinvent their own responses and initiatives from scratch is not necessary. There already are some informal collaborative groups among Christian higher education professionals (e.g., listserv groups), but there may be a need create a more formal focus group to tackle this reality. National groups such as Council for Christian Colleges and Universities (CCCU), Association for Biblical Higher Education (ABHE), Association for Christians in Student Development (ACSD), National Christian College Athletic Association (NCCAA), and others may be organizations that are equipped and poised to organize such a group.

The group can involve using a listserv to communicate to others from different institutions. This is a great way to tap into a network of experienced professionals. If there is a specific situation that arises on campus, post a question on the listserv to glean from the experiences of others. In addition, this group could coordinate monthly webinars or teleconferences. Each webinar or teleconference could feature a speaker or expert on sexuality to train and equip professionals in Christian higher education. At the end of each webinar or teleconference, a question-and-answer time along with discussion would undoubtedly be beneficial for the members of this group. Members of this group could include student development staff, residence life staff, administration, and even faculty. Many other opportunities and brainstorming potentials exist for creatively linking up with those who perform similar roles at other schools, asking each other questions about how situations are being handled on their campuses and what can be learned from each others' mistakes, victories, and other lessons.

33. *Educating constituency*

Often forgotten in the day-to-day of many students on campus is that the community of the college or university actually extends far beyond the physical campus. Its brand, reputation, identity, and principles are strongly impacted by individuals who are not carrying books and papers to class everyday. These constituencies include alumni, donors, parents, local churches, and other groupings of people who bear an affiliation of some kind with the school. When trying to change the culture of an institution, efforts must be made to train, equip, and share information with these key assortments and demographics, perhaps through alumni magazines and correspondence, through donor events, and other available means that are representative of each individual college. When addressing these issues of sexuality, be sure to closely work with the alumni relations office and the donor relations office, because these two offices are the closest to the school's constituency. Keep them informed during the planning of any statements or events in which constituency may have an opinion about. In addition, the alumni relations and donor relations offices would be very knowledgeable with ways in which to equip and educate the people that they interact with. Alumni and donor events can be a good way to inform them about LGB and SSA students on campus.

34. Assessment

One final action step would be to assess how well a school is doing in reducing marginalization of LGB and SSA students. This can bring to light any weaknesses that may need attention. Evaluations are important to avoid blind spots that can develop and to get a sense of the campus climate from the students themselves. An external group can conduct the assessment. An online anonymous survey can be utilized similar to this study's questionnaire.

Be a Pallet Bearer

In Mark 2:1-12, Jesus was preaching in a home in Capernaum and because word had spread, a horde of people gathered to see and hear this new teacher who performed miracles. Four men also came bringing their paralyzed friend. The passage provides no description of the four friends. There is no hint as to where they had come or what was their place in society. In addition, there are no descriptors for the paralyzed man. How did he talk his friends into bringing him? Or was this all his friends' idea? As they approached, they realized the problem—the near impenetrable crowd of people. Most would have given up and turned around after seeing the dense thicket of women and men gathered around the house where Jesus was teaching. It would take too much effort to bring their paralyzed friend to even get near the teacher. And even if the four friends tried, there was no guarantee that Jesus would take notice of them. However, they did not give up. They pressed forward and persevered. A hole was dug through the mud and thatch roof and the paralyzed man was lowered on a pallet. Four friends were determined to do whatever it took to bring their friend to the foot of Jesus.

The research revealed that many LGB and SSA students felt a need to hide their sexuality. For whatever reason, they did not feel that their campus was a safe place to process with others. Many were immobilized by fear and by the stigma they perceived on campus. In essence, they were paralyzed and their isolation could have prevented them from seeking Jesus. What paralyzed people need most are people who will be friends,

friends who will pallet bearers. These are friends who do not give up easily, friends who are relentless. The Gospel of Mark records Jesus' reaction. He did not react to the faith of the paralyzed man, but he was amazed at the faith of the four friends (Mark 2:5). Professionals at Christian colleges and universities should make it a priority to be a friend and/or improve the campus culture by encouraging sacrificial friendship. God would be glorified when Christian college and university campuses are full of friends who are pallet bearers.

---— Appendix A —---

Questionnaire

Demographic information (page 1 of 3 of questionnaire)

B1. Age:

☐ [Select from pull-down menu]

B2. Sex:

☐ Male

☐ Female

☐ Other [Fill in the blank]

B3. What is your race? (check all that apply)

☐ Caucasian

☐ African-American or African descent

☐ Hispanic

☐ Asian

☐ Native American

☐ Pacific Islander

☐ Other [Fill in the blank]

B4. Are you a current student or alumnus/alumna of a Christian college or university?

☐ Current student

☐ Alumnus/alumna

☐ I attended for at least one full year but never graduated

☐ I attended for less than one full year but never graduated

B5. What is the name of the Christian college or university that you currently attend or attended?

☐ [Select from pull-down menu]

If not listed above, please type in the name of the Christian college or university that you currently attend or did attend.

☐ Other [Fill in the blank]

B6. When will you or did you graduate from this Christian college or university?

☐ [Select from pull-down menu]

If you did not graduate, what was the last year you attended this Christian college or university?

☐ Last year (e.g., 2010) [Fill in the blank]

B7. As a college or university student, are you living or did you live in the residence halls?

☐ Yes

☐ No

B8. How would you describe yourself now as a sexual minority?

☐ Gay or lesbian

☐ Person with same-sex attractions

☐ Bisexual

☐ Gay and celibate

☐ Other [Fill in the blank]

B9. As a college or university student, how many know you are or knew you were a sexual minority?

☐ Nobody

☐ A select few

☐ As a student, I am or was fairly open about my sexuality

B10. As a college or university student, why are or were you open or not open about your sexuality?

☐ [Block area to answer open-ended question]

B11. For the majority of the time as a college or university student, please indicate what is or was your relationship status?

☐ Single and not dating

☐ Casually dating

☐ Seriously dating

☐ Engaged/Married

☐ Other [Fill in the blank]

Sexual Minority Student Experience
(page 2 of 3 of questionnaire)

C1. Describe any positive and/or negative experiences you've had as a sexual minority, college or university student in the residence halls.

☐ [Block area to answer open-ended question]

C2. Describe any positive and/or negative experiences you've had as a sexual minority, college or university student in the classroom.

☐ [Block area to answer open-ended question]

C3. Describe any positive and/or negative experiences you've had as a sexual minority, college or university student as you interacted with your classmates.

☐ [Block area to answer open-ended question]

C4. Describe any positive and/or negative experiences you've had as a sexual minority, college or university student, which were not covered above.

☐ [Block area to answer open-ended question]

C5. What type of chapel messages or student programming which focused on singleness were available to you as a college or university student? Describe how this was helpful or not helpful.

☐ [Block area to answer open-ended question]

C6. What type of chapel messages or student programming which focused on sexuality were available to you as a college or university student? Describe how this was helpful or not helpful.

☐ [Block area to answer open-ended question]

C7. I am aware of what my college or university's lifestyle agreement says about homosexuality.

☐ Yes   ☐ No   ☐ Don't know

C8. I am aware that my college or university has an additional statement on homosexuality which is in addition to the lifestyle agreement.

☐ Yes, I am aware ☐ There's no additional statement ☐ I am not aware

Please indicate the degree to which you agree with the following statements.

C9. I believe God blesses monogamous unions between two people of the same sex (i.e., it is NOT a sin).	Agree	Some-what agree	Some-what dis-agree	Dis-agree	Don't know
C10. I agree with my college or university's lifestyle agreement on homosexuality.	Agree	Some-what agree	Some-what dis-agree	Dis-agree	Don't know
C11. As a student, my college or university's lifestyle agreement on homosexuality makes or made me feel marginalized and/or unsafe.	Agree	Some-what agree	Some-what dis-agree	Dis-agree	Don't know

C12. I agree with my college or university's additional statement on sexuality which is in addition to the lifestyle agreement. (If your school doesn't have one, leave this blank).	Agree	Some-what agree	Some-what dis-agree	Dis-agree	Don't know

C13. Explain why you agree or disagree with your college or university's statement(s) on homosexuality.

☐ [Block area to answer open-ended question]

For the following questions, please indicate the degree to which you feel or felt as a sexual minority college or university student.

C14. How often do or did you feel that you lacked companionship as a sexual minority, college or university student?	Hardly ever	Some-times	Often
C15. How often do or did you feel left out as a sexual minority, college or university student?	Hardly ever	Some-times	Often
C16. How often do or did you feel isolated from others as a sexual minority, college or university student?	Hardly ever	Some-times	Often

Recommendations (page 3 of 3 of questionnaire)

D1. What recommendations would you give to faculty and administration on how they can make your college or university a healthier environment for sexual minority students to grow and thrive in their Christian faith?

☐ [Block area to answer open-ended question]

D2. What recommendations would you give to residence life and student development staff on how they can make your college or university a healthier environment for sexual minority students to grow and thrive in their Christian faith?

☐ [Block area to answer open-ended question]

D3. What recommendations would you give to other college or university students on how they can make your college or university a healthier environment for sexual minority students to grow and thrive in their Christian faith?

☐ [Block area to answer open-ended question]

D4. What can your college or university do to communicate that it is a healthy and safe environment for sexual minority students before they even arrive on campus?

☐ [Block area to answer open-ended question]

Thank you very much for your valuable input in this project! Again, your participation has been completely anonymous and your demographic data will remain confidential as well. Comments or questions about this project and/or questionnaire can be directed to me, Christopher Yuan (principal investigator) at cy@christopheryuan.com, or Dr. Katie Friesen Smith (thesis advisor).

—— Appendix B ——
Informed Consent Form

Introduction

You are invited to participate in a qualitative study on the experiences of sexual minority students at Christian colleges and universities. I (Christopher Yuan, principal investigator) hope to learn how Christian colleges and universities can improve in creating a healthy place for sexual minority students to grow and thrive in their Christian faith. This research project is for my final thesis in partial fulfillment of the doctorate of ministry program at Bethel Seminary in St. Paul, MN.

Procedures

If you agree to participate in this study, you will be asked to answer a series of questions, beginning with some demographic questions, followed by some open-ended questions on your experiences as a sexual minority student, and finally you will be asked for recommendations on how your Christian college or university can improve in making the campus a healthier place for sexual minority students to grow and thrive in their Christian faith. The questionnaire may take forty-five minutes or more to complete, depending on how much you decide to share. The more you share, the more beneficial it will be for this study. However, you are free to share as little or as much as you feel comfortable or led to.

Risks/Discomforts

There is a possibility of experiencing negative emotions related to reflecting on being a sexual minority student at a Christian college or university. As with any research, there is some possibility that you may be subject to risks that have not yet been identified. As you fill out the questionnaire, you are free to skip any question (or questions) or discontinue participation in this study without prejudice.

Benefits

There are no direct benefits for participants. However, there are a couple indirect benefits from participating in this study. First, it will provide you an opportunity to reflect on your time at your Christian college or university in light of being a sexual minority. Second, you are helping to contribute to an important area of research that can deeply affect future sexual minority students at Christian colleges and universities.

Confidentiality

Participation in this study and the information collected is completely anonymous. Any information obtained in connection with this study that can be identified with you will remain confidential. All demographic data obtained from participants will be kept confidential and will only be reported in an aggregate format (by reporting only combined results and never reporting individual ones). The name of your Christian college or university will not be released or used in written reports. Only the principal investigator will have access to the data collected from the questionnaires. The data collected from the questionnaires will be stored in the HIPPA-compliant, Qualtrics-secure database until it has been deleted by the principal investigator.

Participation

Participation in this research study is completely voluntary. You have the right to withdraw at any time or refuse to participate entirely without prejudice. If you desire to withdraw, simply close your Internet browser.

Questions about the Research

If you have any questions about this study, you may contact me (principal investigator) at cy@christopheryuan.com.

Questions about your Rights as Research Participants

This research project has been reviewed and approved in accordance with Bethel University's Levels of Review for Research with Humans. If you have questions you do not feel comfortable asking the researcher, questions regarding your rights as a research participant, or wish to report a research-related injury, you may contact Dr. Katie Friesen Smith (thesis advisor) at kjsmith@nwc.edu, or Dr. Peter Jankowski (Chairperson of the Bethel University Institutional Review Board) at pjankows@bethel.edu.

If at any time during this study, you experience emotional discomfort, distress, or negative emotions and desire assistance, please contact a licensed clinical professional counselor. If you are a student, please contact the counseling center at your school.

I have read and understand the above consent form and desire of my own free will to participate in this study.

☐ Yes   ☐ No

Appendix C
Principal Contact Letter

Dear Dr. _____:

My name is Christopher Yuan and I am conducting a qualitative study on the experiences of sexual minority students at Christian colleges and universities. This research project is for my final thesis in partial fulfillment of the doctorate of ministry program at Bethel Seminary in St. Paul, MN. My hope is to learn how Christian colleges and universities can maintain a traditional view of sexuality and improve in creating a healthy place for sexual minority students to grow and thrive in their Christian faith.

Do you know of any sexual minority students or alumni who would be interested in participating in this study and able to give some thoughtful reflection on this topic? Students and alumni interested in participating in this study will be directed to the Qualtrics website (a third-party, online survey platform) where they will find a questionnaire which may take forty-five minutes or more to complete. Their participation will be completely anonymous (participants will not be asked to give their name) and confidential (demographic data will only be reported in an aggregate format).

This research project has been reviewed and approved in accordance with Bethel University's Levels of Review for Research with Humans. The data collected on the Qualtrics website will be stored in the HIPPA-compliant, Qualtrics-secure database until it has been deleted by the principal investigator. Qualtrics is an independent, third-party, online survey platform independent from the principal investigator or any academic institution.

The names of participating Christian colleges and universities will not be released or used in written reports.

If you have any students or alumni who you think would be interested in participating, can you give them a copy of the attached "Initial Contact Participant" letter? In this letter will be a link to the Qualtrics website. Below is a link where you can preview the questionnaire. *Note: Do not give this link to students or alumni since it is only for preview. A link for the questionnaire is provided in the attached "Initial Contact Participant" letter.*

https://bethel.qualtrics.com/SE/?SID=SV_4MK2ouR3A1pvdwF&Preview=Survey&BrandID=bethel

If you have questions, feel free to contact me. Thanks so much for your help!

Sincerely,

Christopher Yuan, Principal Investigator

——— Appendix D ———
Potential Participant Letter

Dear Friend:

My name is Christopher Yuan and I am conducting a qualitative study on the experiences of non-heterosexual or sexual minority[1] students at Christian colleges and universities. This research project is for my final thesis in partial fulfillment of the doctorate of ministry program at Bethel Seminary in St. Paul, MN. My hope is to learn how Christian colleges and universities can improve in creating a healthy place for non-heterosexual or sexual minority students to grow and thrive in their Christian faith.

You were asked to consider possibly participating in this study because you are a non-heterosexual or sexual minority student or recent alumnus/alumna (past ten years) of a Christian college or university, and thus able to provide some thoughtful reflection on this topic.

If you are interested in participating in this study, the link at the bottom of this letter will direct you to the Qualtrics website (a third-party, online survey platform). There you will be able to read more information about the study, and after agreeing to what is written in the consent form, you may begin the questionnaire. The questionnaire may take forty-five minutes or more to complete. If you cannot finish in one sitting, you are

1. For this research project, a sexual minority is defined as one who identifies either as lesbian, gay, or bisexual, or as one who experiences same-sex attractions (and may not embrace a gay identity). This term seems to be more inclusive of both LGB people and people with SSA. Although some may draw a correlation between sexual minorities and racial minorities, no correlation is intended in this research project.

able to save and finish later *as long as you use the same computer and same browser*. Your participation will be completely anonymous (you will not be asked to give your name) and confidential (demographic data will only be reported in an aggregate format).

This research project has been reviewed and approved in accordance with Bethel University's Levels of Review for Research with Humans. The data collected on the Qualtrics website will be stored in the HIPPA-compliant, Qualtrics-secure database until it has been deleted by the principal investigator. Qualtrics is a third-party, online survey platform independent from the principal investigator or any academic institution.

If you have questions, feel free to contact me, my thesis advisor, or the chairperson of the Bethel University Institutional Review Board. Thanks so much for your consideration!

Here is an anonymous survey link to begin the study.

https://bethel.qualtrics.com/SE/?SID=SV_4MK2ouR3A1pvdwF

Undeserving of his grace,

Christopher Yuan, Principal Investigator (cy@christopheryuan.com)
Dr. Katie Friesen Smith, Thesis Advisor
Dr. Peter Jankowski, Chairperson of Bethel University's Institutional Review Board

—— Appendix E ——
Review of the Related Literature

THE RESEARCHER REVIEWED RELEVANT theoretical and research-based literature on the marginalization of LGB and SSA students at Christian colleges and universities. The literature was limited to three areas: (1) the marginalization of LGB and SSA college and university students; (2) recommendations for reducing marginalization of LGB and SSA college and university students; and (3) terminology in research for LGB and SSA college and university students.

Marginalization of LGB and SSA College and University Students

Secular Colleges and Universities

Susan Rankin conducted a national study documenting the experiences of LGBT students, faculty, and staff and their perceptions of the campus climate toward LGBT people.[1] Fourteen colleges and universities participated in this study and 1,669 surveys were completed ($N = 1,669$). Until 2003, no study of its kind had a larger sample utilizing the same assessment tool. Because LGBT students were difficult to identify, purposeful and snowball sampling procedures were utilized. Purposeful sampling was utilized by initially contacting LGBT individuals through LGBT groups or listservs to participate in the study. Snowball sampling was then utilized by asking

1. Rankin, *Campus Climate*, 4.

LGBT individuals who have participated to share the survey with other LGBT individuals who may not have been in any groups or listservs or who may not have disclosed their sexual identity publicly on campus.[2] The survey contained 35 multiple-choice questions regarding (1) respondent's personal campus experiences as an LGBT person; (2) perceptions of the campus climate toward LGBT people; and (3) perceptions of administrative policies and academic initiatives related to LGBT issues. Although graduate students ($n = 281$), staff ($n = 372$), faculty ($n = 150$), and administrators ($n = 95$) participated in this study, the largest cohort of respondents were undergraduate students ($n = 719$). Fifty-two respondents did not report their position.

From this study, Rankin discovered that 19 percent of all the respondents (students, faculty, and staff) feared for their physical safety within the past year because of their sexual orientation or gender identity. To avoid intimidation, 51 percent of all the respondents concealed their sexual orientation or gender identity, and 34 percent avoided disclosing their sexual orientation or gender identity for fear of negative consequences, harassment, or discrimination. Among all the respondents, 29 percent indicated that they experienced harassment due to their sexual orientation or gender identity within the past year. In addition, the subgroup that experienced the most harassment was undergraduate students (36 percent), and the majority of these incidents were from other students (79 percent). Some examples of harassment reported were derogatory remarks (89 percent), verbal harassment or threats (48 percent), and even physical assault (11 respondents).

Although marginalization, harassment, and even assault of LGBT students, faculty, and staff were reported, Rankin stated that the fourteen participating colleges and universities may be among the most "gay-friend-ly" campuses in the country and may not be representative of other colleges and universities.[3] All fourteen participating colleges and universities supported an LGBT office on campus and provided safe space programs. All but one college or university included sexual orientation in their non-discrimination policies, provided benefits for domestic partners and were creating a program for LGBT studies. Rankin was not able to determine the effectiveness of these initiatives because there was no comparable data from before their implementation. It is possible that the situation had been worse

2. Rankin, *Campus Climate*, 6n4.

3. Rankin, *Campus Climate*, 3.

before implementation. It is also possible that these changes elevated LGBT visibility, therefore heightening anti-LGBT sentiments on campus. A third possibility is that these initiatives helped LGBT people to be more confident that they would not face anti-LGBT bias, resulting in an increased reporting of marginalization, harassment, and discrimination.

Although the survey utilized a mixed methods approach, all thirty-five questions were quantitative in nature with space at the end of the survey to add suggestions on how to improve campus climate for LGBT people. Targeted, open-ended questions could have allowed greater input from respondents, allowing the voiceless to have more of a voice. This study did provide some breakdown of the data between students and non-students (faculty and staff); however, not all data showed this distinction between undergraduate students and others. It may have been helpful to provide separation of the data among the different groups of respondents (students and non-students). There also was no differentiation of data between LGB and transgender students.

Robert Brown and colleagues sought to assess the campus climate for LGBT students at the University of Nebraska-Lincoln (UNL).[4] Respondents included LGBT students ($n = 80$), general students ($n = 253$), faculty members ($n = 126$), student affairs staff members ($n = 41$) and resident hall assistants ($n = 105$).[5] The total sample size was 605 ($N = 605$). Three distinct surveys were utilized: (1) general students and resident hall assistants; (2) faculty and student affairs staff; and (3) LGBT students. The third survey for LGBT students included questions pertaining to their extent of political and social activity, verbal and physical attacks, perceptions of unfair treatment, need to hide identity, comparison of campus climate to past years, and extent of being out.

All the LGBT student respondents perceived UNL to exhibit anti-LGBT attitudes to some extent, with 47 percent perceiving great or very great anti-LGBT attitudes. In comparison, 74 percent of participants in Rankin's national study believed their campus was homophobic.[6] Two thirds (66 percent) of UNL LGBT student respondents felt the need to hide their sexuality from other students. Nearly a third (30 percent) of LGBT student respondents reported verbal insults in the past academic year, with 21 percent occurring more than once. Similar to Rankin's 2003 national

4. Brown et al., "Report: Campus Climate and Needs Assessment Study."
5. Brown et al., "Assessing the Campus Climate," 8.
6. Brown and Gortmaker, "Comparing the UNL Campus Climate."

survey, the UNL study found that most of the derogatory remarks about LGBT people were made by other students. Although none had reported being physically assaulted, three percent had been threatened with physical violence and nine percent had personal property damaged or destroyed. Some LGBT respondents stated that they did not report verbal abuse or physical threats to their school because they did not want to "escalate" the situation or did not know how or where to make a report. LGBT students felt that the climate in the residence halls was not positive and were often eager to move out.

Susan Longerbeam and colleagues performed a secondary analysis of data collected from a 2004 national living–learning program study to better understand the broader college experiences of LGB students, particularly their broader academic, cocurricular, and social involvements.[7] To balance the size of the subgroups for statistical analysis, the full subgroup of 52 lesbians was used and random samples were selected from the other subgroups (55 gay men, 55 bisexual men, 55 bisexual women, 55 heterosexual men, and 55 heterosexual women). The total sample size was 327 ($N = 327$). Longerbeam and colleagues discovered that LGB students did not perceive a more hostile climate in residence halls than their heterosexual counterparts. However, since a large majority of the sample were freshmen students (51.4 percent), they may not have had enough experience in the residence hall to label it as hostile. Longerbeam and colleagues stated a limitation of this study was that it only gathered data from students who self-identified as LGB. Therefore, the experiences of those who are SSA but do not identify as LGB were not gathered.[8]

Although other campus climate research concentrated on explicit anti-LGB acts (harassment, verbal threats, or physical assault), Perry Silverschanz and colleagues investigated the more subtle forms of homophobia and heterosexism in higher education. They undertook one of the first studies of heterosexist experiences from both LGB students and heterosexual students.[9] By including both LGB and heterosexual students, the experiences of those invisible LGB students who were not "out" may have been included. In addition, Silverschanz and colleagues compared the results between heterosexual students and LGB students. Differences could be due to LGB students experiencing more homophobia and heterosexism

7. Longerbeam et al., "Lesbian, Gay, and Bisexual College Student Experiences," 217.

8. Longerbeam et al., 221.

9. Silverschanz et al., "Slurs, Snubs, and Queer Jokes," 179.

Appendix E

than heterosexual students. Differences may also be due to LGB students perceiving situations differently than their straight classmates or LGB students supportive of LGB activism providing biased responses.

The participating institution was a small public university in the northwest U.S. The final sample of undergraduate and graduate students was 3,128 (N = 3,128) with 11 percent (n = 351) identifying as lesbian, gay, bisexual, or between bisexual and heterosexual ("mostly heterosexual"). Silverschanz and colleagues referred to this group of 11 percent as "sexual minorities." The "mostly heterosexual" group consisted of 252 respondents, and LGB students (n = 99) actually represented only 3 percent of the total sample size. To avoid possible bias, questions pertaining to psychological and academic well-being were placed before questions pertaining to heterosexist harassment. The survey was administered via the Internet and consisted of quantitative questions regarding psychological well-being, academic well-being, and heterosexist harassment.

Among all respondents, 41 percent reported some experience of heterosexist harassment. Heterosexist harassment was defined as "insensitive verbal and symbolic (but non-assaultive) behaviors that convey animosity toward non-heterosexuality."[10] Among subgroups, 39 percent of heterosexual students (n = 1,077) and 57 percent of sexual minority students (n = 195) reported that they experienced or witnessed heterosexist harassment. A distinction was made between "personal" heterosexist harassment and "ambient" heterosexist harassment. Personal heterosexist harassment was "directly targeted acts, such as being called 'dyke' to one's face."[11] Ambient heterosexist harassment was "actions that take place within the environment but are not directed at a specific target, such as the telling of anti-LGB jokes that can be heard by anyone within earshot."[12] Among sexual minority students, 47 percent experienced personal heterosexist harassment and 53 percent experienced ambient heterosexist harassment. Among heterosexual students, 16 percent reported personal heterosexist harassment and 84 percent described ambient heterosexist harassment. It was not clear whether the respondents were actual victims or witnesses of personal heterosexist harassment.

10. Silverschanz et al., 180.

11. Silverschanz et al., 180.

12. Silverschanz et al., 180.

Funded by Campus Pride, the leading national nonprofit organization working to create a safer college environment for LGBT students,[13] Susan Rankin and colleagues completed the most comprehensive national research of its kind to date and published in 2010.[14] A total of 5,149 surveys were completed by students, staff members, faculty members, and administrators from all 50 states and all Carnegie Basic Classifications of Institutions of Higher Education ($N = 5,149$). Respondents reported their gender identity accordingly: (a) 38 percent man; (b) 48 percent woman; (c) 3 percent transmasculine; (d) 2 percent transfeminine; and (e) 8 percent other. Respondents reported their sexual identity accordingly: (a) 33 percent gay or similar; (b) 20 percent lesbian or similar; (c) 12 percent bisexual, not lesbian, gay or queer; (d) 16 percent queer; (e) 16 percent heterosexual; and (f) 2 percent asexual. The majority of respondents (75 percent) were "out" to their friends regarding their sexual identity.

Although Longerbeam and colleagues did not find that LGB students reported a more hostile climate in residence halls than their heterosexual counterparts, Rankin and colleagues discovered that lesbian, gay, bisexual, and queer (LGBQ) respondents (23 percent) were more likely to experience harassment than heterosexual respondents (12 percent). Heterosexual respondents were half as likely (29 percent) to be targets of derogatory remarks as LGBQ respondents (61 percent). Racial minority LGBQ respondents encountered multiple forms of oppression and were ten times as likely (20 percent) to indicate racial profiling as Caucasian LGBQ respondents (2 percent). LGBQ respondents perceived the campus climate to be more negative and less comfortable than heterosexual respondents. Rankin and colleagues also discovered that LGBQ students, faculty, and staff often considered leaving their institution, avoided areas of campus where LGBQ people were known to congregate, avoided disclosure of their sexual identity due to intimidation or negative consequences, and feared for their physical safety as a result of their sexual identity. Because the recruitment strategy was convenience sampling and not random sampling, it may have resulted in selection bias. Leading questions in the survey may also have invoked response bias.

The literature related to the marginalization of LGB and SSA students at secular colleges and universities fell into five general themes. The first theme was that LGB and SSA students perceived the campus climate to

13. Campus Pride, "About."

14. Rankin et al., *2010 State of Higher Education*, 8.

be negative. The second theme was that LGB and SSA students concealed their sexual orientation. The third theme was that LGB and SSA students reported harassment (personal and ambient) and some even reported fear for their physical safety in spite of being at some of the most "gay friendly" campuses in the country. The fourth theme was that the greatest source of harassment reported by LGB and SSA students was from other students. The fifth theme was that in spite of all these institutions not having institutional policies against same-sex sexual practice and not being Christian institutions, marginalization of LGB and SSA students was still present. Marginalization was not unique to Christian colleges and universities and the absence of institutional policies did not solve the problem of marginalization of LGB and SSA students.

Christian Colleges and Universities

Joel Wentz and Roger Wessel sought to understand the experiences of gay and lesbian students at Christian colleges and universities and to find ways to improve campus climate for gay and lesbian students.[15] The methodology was qualitative and phenomenological in nature. One of the researchers had personal contacts who were gay or lesbian at different Christian institutions. The participants were five gay and three lesbian students from four Christian institutions, ranging from sophomores to seniors ($N = 8$). None identified as gay or lesbian before attending college. All eight participants no longer believe that same-sex sexual practice and romantic relationships are sinful. Although all started college as Christians, at the time of the study one identified as atheist, four no longer identified as Christian, and three still identified as a Christian. All respondents believed that same-sex relationships were not sinful.

Semi-structured interviews were conducted in person. The proposed interview guide was reviewed and piloted. Upon analyzing the data, Wentz and Wessel discovered five main findings regarding the experiences of the participants. First, although all experienced same-sex attractions before attending college, they all indicated a time of denying the possibility of accepting a gay or lesbian identity. Three reported that they chose a Christian college or university in the hopes of not becoming or identifying as gay or lesbian. Second, each student expressed that the campus climate was extremely negative. One respondent stated that he would hear people say

15. Wentz and Wessel, "Experiences of Gay and Lesbian Students," 42.

"faggot" or make fun of gays. Three participants identified their professors as a source of anti-gay sentiment. Third, several participants stated that exposure to off-campus culture was significant in the development of their sexual identity. Fourth, all eight students felt pressure to hide their sexual identity while on campus after they had accepted being gay or lesbian. They feared losing their on-campus job, being fined, being forced into mandatory counseling sessions, or being suspended. Respondents reported a pervasive feeling of anxiety and feared that someone would find out. Fifth, the participants all attempted to reconcile their Christian faith and their gay or lesbian identity. Three maintained their Christian faith while the other five did not.

Wentz and Wessel also found five influences that positively or negatively affected the respondents' experiences. First, support from faculty and staff who held to a progressive view of sexuality (PVS) was an extremely positive aspect of their experience. One student reported that faculty and staff would give him secret notes stating that they did not think homosexuality was a sin and then requested the note be ripped up. Another participant stated that a Bible professor gave her resources on alternative biblical interpretations. Second, four students sought help from the counseling center and each stated that their experience was positive. Their counselors did not pressure them to change or ignore their sexuality. One student reported that his counselor did not believe homosexuality was a sin. Third, the participants overwhelmingly had a negative perception of the student handbook and institutional policies. One student reported that according to the handbook, it was okay to be gay, just do not "do anything gay."[16] The respondents perceived that the policies placed an extra emphasis upon homosexuality and were a double standard with many violations receiving little discipline while homosexuality was more severely punished.

Fourth, Wentz and Wessel found that the male residence hall culture was negative, foreign, and intimidating. What was supposed to be humorous was often offensive and immature. For example, one male participant reported that the guys would wrestle naked and take showers together. Fifth, the respondents' perception of administrators was exceedingly negative. The students felt the administrators were ignorant and out of touch. One gay participant was pulled from summer tour when another student told university administrators that he was gay. Although it is important to listen to the perspectives of these students, Wentz and Wessel only

16. Wentz and Wessel, 49.

interviewed gay and lesbian students in disagreement with the institutional policies on homosexuality. The voices of LGB and SSA students in agreement with the institutional policies on homosexuality were not included in this study and these voices of less "out" students are often unheard. With such a limited sample size, the findings of Wentz and Wessel should not be viewed as representative of all LGB and SSA students at Christian colleges and universities.

Mark Yarhouse and colleagues investigated two areas in their 2009 study: milestone events in sexual identity development and campus climate for sexual minorities at Christian colleges and universities.[17] This pilot study gathered data from 104 respondents at three Christian institutions who experienced same-sex attractions ($N = 104$). An online, anonymous questionnaire was developed to target those unheard or unrecognized voices. Anonymity provided safety so that respondents could participate without being identified. Yarhouse and colleagues employed a mixed methods approach of quantitative and qualitative (grounded theory) methodologies. Related to milestone events, participants were asked about their early experiences with same-sex attractions, their family background, their disclosure to family and friends about same-sex attractions, their sexual experiences, and their religious coping.

The participants reported the campus climate of their schools to be negative overall. According to 84 percent of respondents, the campus view of homosexuality was "generally negative" or "negative," while 96 percent stated that the campus view of homosexual behavior was also "generally negative" or "negative."[18] From the students' responses, this negative campus climate was generally not due to faculty or staff. It was other students that were identified to be the major influence of a negative campus atmosphere, with 96 percent hearing derogatory speech in the presence of their peers. More male respondents (87 percent) than female respondents (59 percent) reported a negative comment from their peers at least four times during the past year. Negative comments were typically heard among peers in social settings and less often by faculty and staff. Male students seemed more likely to hear derogatory comments but were less likely to view it as problematic.

Yarhouse and colleagues found that the majority of respondents had not yet disclosed their sexuality with their family. Approximately 75 percent

17. Yarhouse et al., "Listening to Sexual Minorities," 96.
18. Yarhouse et al., "Listening to Sexual Minorities," 104.

had not disclosed to their mothers, 82 percent had not disclosed to their fathers, and 85 percent had not disclosed to their siblings. Respondents did open up more with friends, 42 percent. But even this percentage seemed low "relatively speaking."[19] Both teachers and youth pastors were the least likely to know about the respondents' sexuality (both at 93 percent).

Yarhouse and colleagues asked participants about their awareness and usage of campus resources. Awareness ranged from 75 percent for counseling services, to 57 percent for faculty and staff, to 39 percent for campus ministries, to 54 percent for resident life, and the lowest was 31 percent for student development. Usage ranged from 14 percent for counseling services, to 8 percent for faculty and staff, to 6 percent for resident life, to 2 percent for campus ministries, and 0 percent for student development.

Stephen Stratton and colleagues surveyed 247 students who currently experience or at some point experienced same-sex attractions ($N = 247$). Their report was published in 2013. The participants were from 19 Christian colleges and universities in 14 states.[20] Questions covered attitudes regarding sexuality, sexual identity, religiosity, and sexual milestone events. Although the broader culture perceives LGB and SSA students at Christian colleges and universities to be "either in denial, or terribly repressed, resulting in an arrested or delayed identity development, attributed to in large measure the negative environment in which they find themselves," Stratton and colleagues found that the LGB and SSA respondents were largely conservative, suggesting congruence between their personal beliefs and the beliefs and behavioral expectation of their schools. The sample of SSA students was not monolithic in their perspectives on sexuality and religion.

> This diverse group hopes for a Christian college or university where they can engage identity-based concerns—a general characteristic of this developmental period. Some appear to want a more open process, while others appear to want a more private experience.[21]

A unique aspect of Stratton and colleagues' research when compared to other LGB research was that not only did their participants tend not to pursue same-sex behavior and relationships, but most of their participants chose not to take on a gay identity. The students were asked about their public sexual identity and private sexual identity. A public sexual

19. Yarhouse et al., "Listening to Sexual Minorities," 102.

20. Stratton et al., 3.

21. Stratton et al., 21.

identity would be one's sexual identity openly portrayed on campus to classmates, faculty, and staff. A private sexual identity would be how one views herself or himself. It was discovered that respondents' public and private sexual identities did not always match. Although all respondents currently experience or at some point experienced same-sex attractions, the vast majority of respondents (93.7 percent) claimed a public heterosexual sexual identity, and 71.5 percent of respondents reported both a heterosexual public and private sexual identity. One limitation of this study was that it did not focus on the campus climate for LGB and SSA students.

The literature related to the marginalization of LGB and SSA students at Christian colleges and universities fell into eight general themes. The first theme was that the overall campus climate of Christian colleges and universities was very negative toward LGB and SSA students. The second theme was that LGB and SSA students felt the need to hide their sexual identity. The third theme was that the majority of derogatory remarks were from other students. The fourth theme was that LGB and SSA students attempted to reconcile their faith and sexuality, with some maintaining a traditional view of sexuality (TVS), some changing to a PVS, and some leaving the Christian faith. The fifth theme was that institutional policies on homosexuality were confusing to LGB and SSA students. The sixth theme was that there is a paucity of research on campus climate toward LGB and SSA students at Christian colleges and universities. Therefore, there is a great need for more research in this area. Seventh, the LGB and SSA students at Christian colleges and universities are not monolithic. Eight, LGB and SSA students at Christian colleges and universities had public and private sexual identities.

Reducing Marginalization of LGB and SSA College and University Students

Secular Colleges and Universities

In order to reduce marginalization of LGBT students, faculty, and staff, Rankin suggested that institutions must first shift basic assumptions, premises, and beliefs. For example, "heterosexist assumptions [must be] replaced by assumptions of diverse sexualities."[22] Suggestions were grouped into five

22. Rankin, *Campus Climate*, 41.

categories: (1) actively recruit and retain LGBT administrators, faculty, staff, and students; (2) demonstrate visible institutional commitment to LGBT issues and concerns; (3) integrate LGBT issues into the curriculum; (4) provide educational programming on LGBT issues such as in residence life and student development; and (5) create safe spaces for dialogue and interaction.[23]

From the UNL campus climate study, Brown and colleagues provided recommendations to four levels of leadership at colleges and universities. First, administration should issue a policy that supports improving the campus climate for LGBT people and promote diversity for all. In addition, administration should develop strategies to recruit and retain LGBT faculty and staff. Second, faculty should work to infuse LGBT topics into course content when appropriate and consider developing a minor in LGBT studies. Third, student affairs staff should consider using LGBT student presentations during new student orientation and create safe spaces on campus for LGBT students. Fourth, those in leadership over staffing should hire a full-time campus resource director for LGBT students, which is now recognized as a professional position within student affairs.[24] Although Brown and colleagues did not have access to the results of Rankin's national study at the time, many of their suggestions were very similar.

Nancy Evans and Ellen Broido conducted in-depth interviews with ten lesbian and bisexual women university students.[25] Many expressed that the residence hall climate was generally hostile toward LGB students, but they also reported supportive factors that positively influenced the residence hall environment. Some of these factors were the presence of "out" LGB resident assistants and the confrontation of homophobic remarks by staff, resident assistants, and other students. Halls that were more academically oriented seemed to help improve the residence hall climate. In addition, visible signs and symbols of support and programming about LGB issues helped to create an environment that seemed less hostile and more supportive of LGB students. Supportive roommates were also an important factor in a more positive residence hall experience.

In the 2010 national study, Rankin and colleagues provided many suggestions, which fell into seven broad categories. First, develop inclusive policies that explicitly welcome lesbian, gay, bisexual, transgender, queer,

---

23. Rankin, *Campus Climate*, 42–45.

24. Brown et al., "Executive Summary and Recommendations."

25. Evans and Broido, "The Experiences of Lesbian and Bisexual Women," 29–30.

or questioning (LGBTQQ) students, faculty, and staff. Second, demonstrate institutional commitment by integrating LGBTQQ concerns into all aspects of the institution, such as creating inclusive wording in institutional policies and documents. Third, integrate LGBTQQ issues and concerns in curricular and co-curricular education. Homophobia and heterosexism are often learned in social settings, and exposing students to new ideas and sources of knowledge in co-curricular activities is important. Fourth, respond appropriately to anti-LGBTQQ incidents and bias. Students should be able to feel safe on campus and be able to speak out about incidents of harassment without fear of reprisal. Fifth, create brave spaces for civil dialogue in on-campus housing between LGBTQQ and non-LGBTQQ students. Sixth, offer comprehensive counseling and healthcare. Because of the effects of a negative campus climate (whether perceived or actual), there is a need for counseling support. Seventh, improve recruitment and retention efforts of LGBTQQ students, faculty, and staff.[26]

The literature related to reducing marginalization of LGB and SSA students at secular colleges and universities fell into five general themes. The first theme was to actively recruit and retain LGB administrators, faculty, staff, and students. The second theme was to create institutional policies that support LGB issues and concerns. The third theme was to integrate LGB issues into curricular and co-curricular education. The fourth theme was to create safe spaces for dialogue and interaction. The fifth theme was to respond appropriately to anti-LGB incidents and bias.

Christian Colleges and Universities

Wentz and Wessel interviewed eight students from four Christian institutions, and from the findings, they suggested five recommendations for improving practice. First, applicants with same-sex attractions should carefully approach enrollment decisions because "feelings of same-sex attraction will likely have a negative impact on their collegiate experience."[27] Wentz and Wessel suggested that Christian colleges and universities must be candid with student applicants and family members regarding institutional policies against homosexual behavior. However, this would seem to place an overemphasis on homosexuality, and the respondents complained of perceiving an extra-emphasis on homosexuality. Second,

26. Rankin et al., *2010 State*, 15–17.

27. Wentz and Wessel, 51.

since sexual identity formation often occurs during the college years, gay and lesbian students at Christian colleges and universities should seek exposure to off-campus cultures to assist their sexual identity development. Third, multiple viewpoints on biblical interpretations and the Christian faith should be available to students to help gay and lesbian students reconcile their faith and sexual identity.

Fourth, Wentz and Wessel suggested that administrators should support networks for gay and lesbian students that affirmed a PVS. These supportive networks can consist of faculty, staff, counselors, and other students. This may be difficult for administrators since they often embody the values of their institutions. But administrators can listen to the experiences of gay and lesbian students, encourage supportive counseling, and be honest about their desire to help even though they are restricted due to their position at the institution. Fifth, administrators should realize that institutional policies on homosexual behavior are perceived by gay and lesbian students to be intolerant and confusing. Administrators should realize the importance of continually revising and updating institutional policies. Many of the suggestions from the previous section on secular colleges and universities would be appropriate for those institutions, but at Christian colleges and universities, those suggestions may not be congruous with their doctrines of faith and understanding of LGB issues. Because all eight respondents disagreed with their institutional policies on homosexuality, Wentz and Wessel's suggestions would also not be congruent with the doctrines of most Christian institutions.

Yarhouse and colleagues asked participants of their study to provide specific recommendations to the local church on how to support SSA people. Three themes emerged from the data. First, realize that same-sex attractions are a result of the Fall and should not be sanctioned as normative. Second, understand that homosexuality is equal to other sins. Third, talk more about homosexuality and provide support groups for SSA people. These recommendations can apply to staff and students at Christian colleges and universities. The respondents were also asked what advice they would offer to another SSA student or incoming freshman. Yarhouse and colleagues gave eight suggestions from the participants. First, talk to trusted friends and mentors and do not walk the path alone. Second, pray and ask God for help in overcoming sin. Third, persevere, keep struggling, and do not give up. Fourth, know that you are not alone or unloved. Fifth, healing is possible. Sixth, identify the cause of attraction. If rejection is an issue, seek others of the same sex who are accepting and develop friendships with them. Seventh, do not let same-sex attractions define you. Eighth, study and make your own decisions.[28]

Janet Dean and colleagues studied same-sex attraction attitudes and experiences. This study was part of a broader quantitative study on religiosity, sexual attitudes, and sexual behaviors of Christian college students.[29] The broader study involved 19 Christian colleges and universities from 14 states and utilized an online, anonymous questionnaire with 2,360 students responding and 1,957 completed surveys. Regarding sexual orientation, 96.4 percent ($n = 2,225$, $N = 2,307$) were heterosexual, 0.9 percent ($n = 21$) bisexual, 0.8 percent ($n = 19$) homosexual, 0.2 percent ($n = 5$) transsexual, 1.6 percent ($n = 37$) preferred not to answer, while 59 respondents skipped the question. In a later section of the online questionnaire, participants were also asked if they had ever experienced same-sex attractions, with 11.9 percent ($n = 245$) responding affirmatively.

Dean and colleagues suggested that institutional policies on homosexual behavior must be pastorally sensitive. A policy that condemns homosexual practice may be correct on the surface, "however, it is more complicated when we consider how to help the student who is navigating sexual identity questions and concerns as a follower of Christ."[30] In addition, these institutional policies most likely require explanation in a supportive manner reflecting an awareness and understanding of the experiences of LGB and SSA students. These students also need support and resources to assist them in their identity development, especially when their religious identity conflicts with their sexual identity. Support and resources can include forums for campus-wide discussion, panels on human sexuality, training of student development, student life and residence life staff, support groups offered through the counseling center, etc.

Stratton and colleagues noted that the most vocal LGB advocacy groups often place pressure on institutions to change institutional policies on homosexuality that do not reflect institutional values or the values of the LGB and SSA students in the study.[31] Policies can be maintained while still creating space among students for spiritual and sexual development

28. Yarhouse et al., "Listening to Sexual Minorities," 107–8.

29. Dean et al., "Same-Sex Attraction," 56.

30. Dean et al., 69.

31. Stratton et al, 21.

to occur. The most helpful policies would be those that do not hinder the emotional and spiritual development of LGB and SSA students who agree with the institutional policies and a TVS. Stratton and colleagues suggested that to better understand the sexualities of students, it was necessary to think beyond the simple dichotomy of opposite-sex attraction and same-sex attraction and even beyond the linear continuum from opposite-sex attraction to same-sex attraction. Rather, their sample reported varying degrees of opposite-sex sexual attractions (low, medium, and high) and same-sex sexual attractions (low, medium, and high). This coexistence of both opposite-sex and same-sex attractions led Stratton and colleagues to utilize two continuums to define and measure opposite-sex attractions and same-sex attractions as independently operating variables.[32]

The literature related to reducing marginalization of LGB and SSA students at Christian colleges and universities fell into five general themes. The first theme was not to overemphasize homosexuality in institutional policies. This sin is not worse than any other sin. The second theme was to clarify institutional policies on homosexuality, which are often confusing to LGB and SSA students. Institutional policies should not hinder the emotional and spiritual development of LGB and SSA students. The third theme was to provide more educational resources on homosexuality, such as support groups, campus-wide discussions and panels, and training for staff and student leaders. The fourth theme was to encourage supportive networks of mentors and friends so that LGB and SSA students would not have to walk the path alone. The fifth theme was that a two-continuum paradigm of opposite-sex attractions and same-sex attractions should be utilized to better understand the sexualities of students.

Terminology in Research for
LGB and SSA College and University Students

Different terminology in research was used to refer to LGB and SSA students at secular colleges and universities. Rankin and colleagues in their 2003 national research studied the campus climate for gay, lesbian, bisexual, and transgender (GLBT) people. In this study, sexual identity (gay, lesbian, and bisexual) and gender identity (transgender) were combined.[33] Brown and colleagues followed the same terminology as Rankin and colleagues

32. Stratton et al, 17.

33. Rankin, *Campus Climate*, 2.

using GLBT.[34] Longerbeam and colleagues chose to concentrate their study on sexual identity (and not gender identity) by limiting their research to LGB college students.[35] Silverschanz and colleagues found that 11 percent of their total sample of undergraduate and graduate students ($n = 3{,}128$) were either lesbian, gay, bisexual, or between bisexual and heterosexual. This group was collectively referred to as "sexual minority" in their study.[36] Rankin and colleagues in their 2010 national study used different acronyms (LGBT, LGBQ, and LGBTQQ) in their report.[37] They also noted that people's "self-described sexual identity may also not always correspond" to their sexual attractions.[38]

Research at Christian colleges and universities also used different terminology to refer to LGB and SSA students. Wentz and Wessel interviewed students who felt same-sex attraction or identified as gay or lesbian.[39] The 2009 research of Yarhouse and colleagues focused on sexual minorities. Borrowed from Lisa Diamond's study on female same-sex sexuality, sexual minority was defined as "individuals with same-sex attractions or behavior, regardless of self-identification."[40] The 2004 research of Yarhouse and colleagues revealed that some sexual minorities identified as gay while others did not.[41] Although Yarhouse and colleagues used "sexual minority" in their 2009 research report, the decision to use the older terminology of "homosexual" and "homosexuality" in the online survey was determined by the gatekeepers of the three Christian institutions. It was believed that "homosexual" and "homosexuality" would be better understood within the subculture of Christian higher education.[42]

Similarly, Dean and colleagues used the terminology of sexual minority as well. They also found that the majority of sexual minority respondents were unlikely to embrace a gay identity and concluded that "reporting a same-sex attraction does not equate with having a gay/lesbian or bisexual

34. Brown et al., "Assessing," 8.

35. Longerbeam, 215.

36. Silverschanz et al., 182.

37. Rankin et al., *2010 State,* 5.

38. Rankin et al., *2010 State,* 48.

39. Wentz and Wessel, 56.

40. Yarhouse et al., "Listening to Sexual Minorities," 98; Diamond, "Female Same-sex Sexuality," 142.

41. Yarhouse et al., "Sexual Identity," 3.

42. Yarhouse et al., "Listening to Sexual Minorities," 99.

identity for these students."[43] Following the same pattern, Stratton and colleagues used sexual minority in their research but found that 71.5 percent of their respondents reported having both public and private identities as heterosexual ($n = 171$).[44] Among Christian college and university students, there were some who identified as LGB while others did not identify as LGB.

> It is simply not accurate to think of SSA in either-or categories. Understanding the complexity involved as one contemplates embracing a gay, lesbian, bisexual, or transgendered identity, might help us to begin and sustain an ongoing dialogue with this group of young people in need of our support.[45]

Researchers used different terminology to refer to college and university students who experienced same-sex attractions. The attempt was to be as inclusive as possible for those who identified as LGB, as well as those who did not identify as LGB yet were SSA.

Summary

In review, the relevant theoretical and research-based literature on the marginalization of LGB and SSA students at Christian colleges and universities revealed the following general themes in three categories. The first category was the marginalization of LGB and SSA college and university students with five general themes emerging from the literature. First, the campus climate was perceived to be very negative for LGB and SSA students. Second, LGB and SSA students felt the need to conceal their sexual identity. Third, other students were the greatest source of derogatory speech. Fourth, institutional policies on homosexuality were confusing to LGB and SSA students. Fifth, there was a paucity of research on campus climate toward LGB and SSA students at Christian colleges and universities.

The second category was reducing marginalization of LGB and SSA college and university students with three general themes emerging from the literature. First, clarify institutional policies on homosexuality that encourage the spiritual and emotional development of LGB and SSA students. Second, provide more curricular and co-curricular educational resources

43. Dean et al., 65.

44. Stratton et al., 9. It seems that this study is a continuation of the Dean et al. study in 2011.

45. Dean et al., 73.

on homosexuality. Third, encourage safe and supportive networks of staff and faculty for LGB and SSA students.

The third category was terminology in research for LGB and SSA college and university students, with two general themes emerging from the literature. First, inclusive acronyms were used, such as GLBT, LGB, LGBT, LGBQ, and LGBTQQ. Second, some sexual minorities identified as gay while others did not. The majority of respondents at Christian colleges and universities were unlikely to embrace a gay identity. Therefore it was necessary to utilize terminology other than LGB, such as "students with same-sex attraction" or "sexual minority."

Bibliography

Advocates for Youth. "Glossary." Advocates for Youth: Rights, Respect, Responsibility. http://www.advocatesforyouth.org/index.php?option=com_content&task=view&id=607&Itemid=177.

American Psychological Association. *Answers to Your Questions: For a Better Understanding of Sexual Orientation and Homosexuality*. http://www.apa.org/topics/sexuality/sorientation.pdf.

Bauer, Walter, et al., eds. *A Greek-English Lexicon of the New Testament and Other Early Christian Literature*. Chicago: University of Chicago Press, 2000.

Begg, Christopher T. "Foreigner." In *Anchor Bible Dictionary*, edited by David Noel Freedman, vol. 2, 829–30. New York: Doubleday, 1992.

Belgau, Ron. "Vocation Roundup." Spiritual Friendship: Musings on God, Sexuality, Relationships. http://spiritualfriendship.org/2013/09/06/vocation-roundup/.

Berlant, Lauren G., and Michael Warner. "Sex in Public." In *Intimacy*, edited by Lauren Berlant, 311–30. Chicago: Chicago University Press, 2000.

Bethel University. "Institutional Review Board." http://www.bethel.edu/academics/irb/.

———. "Levels of Review." http://www.bethel.edu/academics/irb/guidelines/levels-of-review.

Biola University, *Undergraduate Student Handbook & Guide to University Policies*, http://static.biola.edu/studentlife/media/downloads/Handbook/student-handbook-revsept2015c.pdf.

Block, Daniel I. *Deuteronomy*. Grand Rapids: Zondervan, 2012.

Blomberg, Craig L. *1 Corinthians*. Grand Rapids: Zondervan, 1994.

———. *Matthew*. Nashville: Broadman, 1992.

Bock, Darrell L. *Luke: 9:51—24:53*. Grand Rapids: Baker, 1994.

Brown, Francis, et al. *Hebrew and English Lexicon*. Peabody: Hendrickson, 2001.

Brown, Robert D., et al. "Assessing the Campus Climate for Gay, Lesbian, Bisexual, and Transgender (GLBT) Students Using a Multiple Perspectives Approach." *Journal of College Student Development* 45, no. 1 (January 2004) 8–26.

———. "Executive Summary and Recommendations: Campus Climate and Needs Assessment Study for Gay, Lesbian, Bisexual, and Transgender (GLBT) Students at the University of Nebraska-Lincoln: Moving Beyond Tolerance Toward Empowerment." http://www.unl.edu/cglbtc/reports/GLBT%20Executive%20Summary.pdf.

Bibliography

———. "Report: Campus Climate and Needs Assessment Study for Gay, Lesbian, Bisexual, and Transgender (GLBT) Students at the University of Nebraska-Lincoln: Moving Beyond Tolerance Toward Empowerment (November 2002)." http://www.unl.edu/cglbtc/reports/GLBT%20Climate%20Reprt%20w%20Tables.pdf.

——— and Valerie Gortmaker. "Comparing the UNL Campus Climate for GLBT Students with Results from a National Study of Campus Climate." http://www.unl.edu/cglbtc/reports/compwithrankin.shtml.

Bruckner, James K. *Jonah, Nahum, Habakkuk, Zephaniah.* Grand Rapids: Zondervan, 2004.

Bruner, Frederick D. *Matthew: A Commentary: The Churchbook, Matthew 13–28.* Grand Rapids: Eerdmans, 1990.

Burge, Gary M. *John.* Grand Rapids: Zondervan, 2000.

Butterfield, Rosaria Champagne. *Openness Unhindered: Further Thoughts of an Unlikely Convert on Sexual Identity and Union with Christ.* Pittsburgh: Crown & Covenant, 2015.

Calvin, John. *Commentary on a Harmony of the Evangelists: Matthew, Mark and Luke.* Translated by William Pringle. Vol. 3. Grand Rapids: Baker, 1993.

Campus Pride. "About." http://www.campuspride.org/about.

The Center for Relationship Enrichment, John Brown University. "Student Relationships Assessment." http://www.liferelationships.com/sra/sample1.asp.

Cheney, Carol, et al. "Institutionalized Oppression Definitions." http://www.pcc.edu/resources/illumination/documents/institutionalized-oppression-definitions.pdf.

Chrysostom, John. *Homilies on the Gospel of Saint Matthew.* Edited by Philip Schaff. Peabody: Hendrickson, 1995.

Collaborative Institutional Training Initiative. "Home Page." https://www.citiprogram.org/.

Craigie, Peter C. *The Book of Deuteronomy.* Grand Rapids: Eerdmans, 1976.

Creswell, John W. *Qualitative Inquiry and Research Design: Choosing Among Five Traditions.* Thousand Oaks: SAGE, 1998.

——— and Vicki L. Plano Clark. *Designing and Conducting Mixed Methods Research.* Los Angeles: SAGE, 2011.

———, et al. "Advanced Mixed Methods Research Designs." In *Handbook of Mixed Methods in Social and Behavioral Research*, edited by Abbas Tashakkori and Charles Teddlie, 209–40. Thousand Oaks: SAGE, 2003.

Danylak, Barry. *A Biblical Theology of Singleness.* Cambridge: Grove, 2007.

Davies, William D., and Dale C. Allison, Jr. *A Critical and Exegetical Commentary on the Gospel According to Saint Matthew.* Vol. 3. Edinburgh: T and T Clark, 1997.

Dean, Janet B., et al. "Same-Sex Attraction." In *Sexuality, Religiosity, Behaviors, Attitudes: A Look at Religiosity, Sexual Attitudes and Sexual Behaviors of Christian College Students*, edited by Michael D. Lastoria, 56–70. Houghton: Association of Christians in Student Development, 2011.

Demarest, Bruce. *The Cross and Salvation: The Doctrine of Salvation.* Wheaton: Crossway, 1997.

Denzin, Norman K., and Yvonna S. Lincoln. *Collecting and Interpreting Qualitative Materials.* Thousand Oaks: SAGE, 1998.

Diamond, Lisa M. "A Dynamical Systems Approach to the Development and Expression of Female Same-sex Sexuality." *Perspectives on Psychological Science* 2, no. 2 (June 2007) 142–61.

Bibliography

———. *Sexual Fluidity: Understanding Women's Love and Desire.* Cambridge: Harvard University Press, 2009.

Dilley, Patrick. *Queer Man on Campus: A History of Non-Heterosexual College Men, 1945–2000.* New York: Routledge Falmer, 2002.

Eckholm, Erik. "Even on Religious Campuses, Students Fight for Gay Identity." *The New York Times* (April 18, 2011). http://www.nytimes.com/2011/04/19/us/19gays.html.

Evans, Nancy J., and Ellen M. Broido. "The Experiences of Lesbian and Bisexual Women in College Residence Halls: Implications for Addressing Homophobia and Heterosexism." *Journal of Lesbian Studies* 6, no. 3–4 (2002) 29–42.

Ewert, David. *A General Introduction to the Bible: From Ancient Tablets to Modern Translations.* Grand Rapids: Zondervan, 1983.

Fee, Gordon D. *The First Epistle to the Corinthians.* Grand Rapids: Eerdmans, 1987.

Feminism and Women's Studies. "Sexual Identity and Gender Identity Glossary." The EServer. http://feminism.eserver.org/sexual-gender-identity.txt.

France, Richard T. *The Gospel of Matthew.* Grand Rapids: Eerdmans, 2007.

Gallion, Emily and Nancy Coleman. "MSA Letter to Curators Calls for Wolfe's Removal." http://www.themaneater.com/stories/2015/11/9/msa-letter-curators-calls-wolfes-removal/.

Galpaz-Feller, Pnina. "The Widow in the Bible and in Ancient Egypt." *Zeitschrift fur die Alttestamentliche Wissenschaft* 120, no. 2 (2008) 231–53.

Garland, David E. *1 Corinthians.* Grand Rapids: Baker Academic, 2003.

———. *2 Corinthians.* Nashville: Broadman and Holman, 1999.

Gay and Lesbian Alliance Against Defamation. *Media Reference Guide.* 8th ed. http://www.glaad.org/files/MediaReferenceGuide2010.pdf.

Gray, Sherman W. "The Least of My Brothers, Matthew 25:31–46: A History of Interpretation." PhD diss., Catholic University of America, 1987.

Green, Joel B. *The Gospel of Luke.* Grand Rapids: Eerdmans, 1997.

Grudem, Wayne. *Systematic Theology: An Introduction to Biblical Doctrine.* Grand Rapids: Zondervan, 1994.

Haas, Ann P., et al. "Suicide and Suicide Risk in Lesbian, Gay, Bisexual, and Transgender Populations: Review and Recommendations." *Journal of Homosexuality* 58, no. 1 (January 2011) 10–51.

Halperin, David M. *Saint Foucault: Towards a Gay Hagiography.* New York: Oxford University Press, 1995.

Hall, Roberta M., and Bernice R. Sandler. *The Campus Climate: A Chilly One for Women?* Washington, DC: Association for American Colleges, 1982.

Hamilton, Victor P. "יָתוֹם." In *New International Dictionary of Old Testament Theology and Exegesis*, edited by Willem VanGemeren, vol. 2, 570–71. Grand Rapids: Zondervan, 1997.

Hartley, John E. "יתם (ytm)." In *Theological Wordbook of the Old Testament*, edited by R. Laird Harris, Gleason L. Archer, Jr., and Bruce K. Waltke, vol. 1, 419. Chicago: Moody, 1980.

Herek, Gregory M., et al. "Internalized Stigma among Sexual Minority Adults: Insights from a Social Psychological Perspective." *Journal of Counseling Psychology* 56, no. 1 (2009) 32–43.

Holwerda, David E., and Roland K. Harrison. "Orphan." In *The International Standard Bible Encyclopedia*, edited by Geoffrey W. Bromiley, rev. ed., vol. 3, 616–17. Grand Rapids: Eerdmans, 1985.

Bibliography

Johnson, Burke and Lisa A. Turner. "Data Collection Strategies in Mixed Methods Research." In *Handbook of Mixed Methods in Social and Behavioral Research*, edited by Abbas Tashakkori and Charles Teddlie, 297–319. Thousand Oaks: SAGE, 2003.

Kalekin-Fishman, Devorah, ed. *Designs for Alienation: Exploring Diverse Realities.* Jyvaskyla: SoPhi, 1998.

———. "Tracing the Growth of Alienation: Enculturation, Socialization, and Schooling in a Democracy." In *Alienation, Ethnicity, and Postmodernity*, edited by Felix Geyer, 95–106. London: Greenwood, 1996.

Kellerman, Diether. "גור *gûr*." In *Theological Dictionary of the Old Testament*, edited by G. Johannes Botterweck and Helmer Ringgren, vol. 2, 439–49. Grand Rapids: Eerdmans, 1975.

King, Nigel and Christine Horrocks. *Interviews in Qualitative Research.* Los Angeles: SAGE, 2010.

Kitzinger, Celia. "Sexualities." In *Handbook of the Psychology of Women and Gender*, edited by Rhoda K. Unger, 272–85. New York: Wiley, 2001.

Köhler, Ludwig, and Walter Baumgartner. *The Hebrew and Aramaic Lexicon of the Old Testament*. Translated and edited by M. E. J. Richardson. 2 vols. Boston: Brill, 2001.

Leighton, Paul. "Salem Nixes Gordon College Contract." *The Salem News.* http://www.salemnews.com/news/local_news/article_feef4591-26c0-5147-98da-81a7b28070fd.html.

Liefeld, Walter L. *1 and 2 Timothy, Titus.* Grand Rapids: Zondervan, 1999.

Lohfink, Norbert. "Poverty in the Laws of the Ancient Near East and of the Bible." *Theological Studies* 52, no. 1 (March 1991) 34–50.

Longerbeam, Susan D., et al. "Lesbian, Gay, and Bisexual College Student Experiences: An Exploratory Study." *Journal of College Student Development* 48, no. 2 (2007) 215–30.

Lovaas, Karen, and Mercilee M. Jenkins, eds. *Sexualities and Communication in Everyday Life: A Reader.* Thousand Oaks: SAGE, 2007.

Marshall, I. Howard. *The Gospel of Luke: A Commentary on the Greek Text.* Grand Rapids: Eerdmans, 1978.

Mayes, Andrew D. H. *Deuteronomy.* Greenwood: Attic, 1979.

Mayes, Preston L. "The Resident Alien, the Fatherless, and the Widow in Deuteronomy: The Priority of Relationship with Israel's God for Social Benevolence." PhD diss., Trinity Evangelical Divinity School, 2012.

McCartney, Dan G. *James.* Grand Rapids: Baker Academic, 2009.

McGeorge, Christi, and Thomas S. Carlson. "Deconstructing Heterosexism: Becoming an LGB Affirmative Heterosexual Couple and Family Therapist." *Journal of Marital and Family Therapy* 37, no. 1 (January 2011) 14–26.

McKnight, Scot. *1 Peter.* Grand Rapids: Zondervan, 1996.

Mental Health America, "Co-Dependency." http://www.mentalhealthamerica.net/co-dependency.

Merrill, Eugene H. *Deuteronomy.* Nashville: Broadman and Holman, 1994.

Monroe, Irene. "Back-to-School Not Welcoming to All LGBTQ-Students in Massachusetts." *The Huffington Post.* http://www.huffingtonpost.com/irene-monroe/backtoschool-not-welcomin_b_5763166.html.

Moo, Douglas J. *James: An Introduction and Commentary.* Downers Grove: InterVarsity, 1985.

———. *The Letter of James.* Grand Rapids: Eerdmans, 2000.

Bibliography

Morgan, Timothy C. "Sailing into the Storm: Philip Ryken and D. Michael Lindsay on the Challenges in Christian Higher Education." *Christianity Today* (March 7, 2012). http://www.christianitytoday.com/ct/2012/march/challenges-christian-higher-education.html?start=2.

Morris, Leon. *The Gospel According to Matthew.* Grand Rapids: Eerdmans, 1992.

———. *Luke: An Introduction and Commentary.* Leicester: InterVarsity, 1988.

Mulgrew, Ian. "B.C. Supreme Court Rules in Favour of Trinity Western University Law School." *The Vancouver Sun.* http://www.vancouversun.com/news/supreme+court+rules+favour+trinity+western+university+school/11580281/story.html.

Newman, Isadore, et al. "A Typology of Research Purposes and Its Relationship to Mixed Methods." In *Handbook of Mixed Methods in Social and Behavioral Research*, edited by Abbas Tashakkori and Charles Teddlie, 167–88. Thousand Oaks: SAGE, 2003.

Ortega, Oliver. "Lynn Public Schools Sever Relationship with Gordon College." *The Boston Globe.* http://www.bostonglobe.com/metro/2014/08/29/lynn-public-schools-sever-relationship-with-gordon-college/aw1KwO4RGVpn284rR1jTgO/story.html.

Oswalt, John N. *The Book of Isaiah: Chapters 40–66.* New International Commentary on the Old Testament. Grand Rapids: Eerdmans, 1998.

———. *Isaiah.* The NIV Application Commentary. Grand Rapids: Zondervan, 2003.

Owen, John. *Overcoming Sin and Temptation*, edited by Kelly M. Kapic and Justin Taylor. Wheaton: Crossway, 2006.

Pauly, Madison and Becca Andrews. "Campus Protests Are Spreading Like Wildfire." *Mother Jones.* http://www.motherjones.com/politics/2015/11/missouri-student-protests-racism.

Pulliam, Sarah. "Gay Rights Group Targets Christian Colleges." *Christianity Today.* http://www.christianitytoday.com/ct/2006/marchweb-only/110-42.0.html.

Qualtrics. "About Us." http://www.qualtrics.com/about/.

Rankin, Susan R. *Campus Climate for Gay, Lesbian, Bisexual and Transgender People: A National Perspective.* New York: The National Gay and Lesbian Task Force Policy Institute, 2003.

———, Warren J. Blumenfeld, et al. *2010 State of Higher Education for Lesbian, Gay, Bisexual and Transgender People.* Charlotte: Campus Pride, 2010.

Ray, Nicholas. "Lesbian, Gay, Bisexual and Transgender Youth: An Epidemic of Homelessness." http://www.thetaskforce.org/downloads/reports/reports/HomelessYouth_ExecutiveSummary.pdf.

Regents of the University of California, "What is campus climate? Why does it matter?" http://campusclimate.ucop.edu/what-is-campus-climate/.

Ridderbos, Jan. *Deuteronomy.* Grand Rapids: Regency Reference Library, 1984.

Ringgren, Helmer. "יָתוֹם *yāttôm*," In *Theological Dictionary of the Old Testament*, edited by G. Johannes Botterweck and Helmer Ringgren, vol. 6, 477–81. Grand Rapids: Eerdmans, 1975.

Robertson, Amy. "Trinity Western University Ready to Go Back to Court to Defend Law School Graduates." http://www.twu.ca/news/2016/001-lsbc-appeal.html.

Rook, John. "Making Widows: The Patriarchal Guardian at Work." *Biblical Theology Bulletin: A Journal of Bible and Theology* 27, no. 1 (Spring 1997) 10–15.

———. "When Is a Widow Not a Widow? Guardianship Provides an Answer." *Biblical Theology Bulletin* 28, no. 1 (Spring 1998) 4–6.

Russell, Dan, et al. "Developing a Measure of Loneliness." *Journal of Personality Assessment* 42, no. 3 (June 1978) 290–94.

Bibliography

Schmidt, Karl L., et al. "πάροικος, παροικία, παροικέω." In *Theological Dictionary of the New Testament*, vol. 5, edited by Gerhard Kittel, et al. 841–53. Grand Rapids: Eerdmans, 1967.

Scott, Jack B. "אַלְמָנָה ('almānā)." In *Theological Wordbook of the Old Testament*, vol. 1, edited by R. Laird Harris, et al. 47. Chicago: Moody, 1980.

Seesemann, Heinrich. "ὀρφανός." In *Theological Dictionary of the New Testament*, vol. 5, edited by Gerhard Kittel, et al. 487–88. Grand Rapids: Eerdmans, 1967.

Silva, Moisés, ed. *New International Dictionary of New Testament Theology and Exegesis*. Grand Rapids: Zondervan, 2014.

Silver, Hilary. "Social Exclusion: Comparative Analysis of Europe and Middle East Youth." http://www.shababinclusion.org/files/558_file_Silver_Paper_final.pdf.

Silverschanz, Perry, et al. "Slurs, Snubs, and Queer Jokes: Incidence and Impact of Heterosexist Harassment in Academia." *Sex Roles* 58, no. 3–4 (February 2008) 179–91.

Soulforce. "Our Story." http://www.soulforce.org/#!our-story/cfvg.

Stählin, Gustav. "ξένος, ξενία, ξενίζω, ξενοδοχέω, φιλοξενία, φιλόξενος." In *Theological Dictionary of the New Testament*, vol. 5, edited by Gerhard Kittel, et al. 1–36. Grand Rapids: Eerdmans, 1967.

———. "χήρα." In *Theological Dictionary of the New Testament*, vol. 9, edited by Gerhard Kittel et al. 440–65. Grand Rapids: Eerdmans, 1967.

Stein, Robert H. *An Introduction to the Parables of Jesus*. Philadelphia: Westminster, 1981.

———. *Luke*. Nashville: Broadman Press, 1992.

Steinberg, Naomi. "Romancing the Widow: The Economic Distinctions between the *almana*, the *issa-almana*, and the *eset-hammet*." In *God's Word for Our World*, vol. 1, edited by J. Harold Ellens, et al. 327–46. London: T and T Clark, 2004.

Stigers, Harold G. "גּוּר (gûr)." In *Theological Wordbook of the Old Testament*, vol. 1, edited by R. Laird Harris, et al. 155–56. Chicago: Moody, 1980.

Stratton, Stephen P., et al. "Sexual Minorities in Faith-Based Higher Education: A National Survey of Attitudes, Milestones, Identity, and Religiosity." *Journal of Psychology and Theology* 41, no. 1 (2013) 3–23.

Thiselton, Anthony C. *The First Epistle to the Corinthians: A Commentary on the Greek Text*. Grand Rapids: Eerdmans, 2000.

Ullerstam, Lars. *The Erotic Minorities: A Swedish View*. Translated by Anselm Hollo. London: Calder and Boyars, 1967.

Van Houten, Christiana. *The Alien in Israelite Law: A Study of the Changing Legal Status of Strangers in Ancient Israel*. Sheffield: JSOT, 1991.

Van Leeuwen, Cornelius. "אַלְמָנָה." In *New International Dictionary of Old Testament Theology and Exegesis*, vol. 1, edited by Willem VanGemeren, 413–15. Grand Rapids: Zondervan, 1997.

Via, Dan O., and Robert A. J. Gagnon. *Homosexuality and the Bible: Two Views*. Minneapolis: Fortress, 2003.

Wentz, Joel M., and Roger E. Wessel. "Experiences of Gay and Lesbian Students Attending Faith-Based Colleges: Considerations for Improving Practice." *Growth: The Journal of the Association for Christians in Student Development* 11 (Spring 2012) 40–58.

Yarhouse, Mark A. *Homosexuality and the Christian: A Guide for Parents, Pastors, and Friends*. Bloomington, Bethany House, 2010.

Bibliography

————. "Sex Attraction, Homosexual Orientation, and Gay Identity: A Three-Tier Distinction for Counseling and Pastoral Care." *Journal of Pastoral Care and Counseling* 59, no. 3 (Fall 2005) 201–11.

————, et al. "Listening to Sexual Minorities on Christian College Campuses." *Journal of Psychology and Theology* 37, no. 2 (2009) 96–113.

————, et al. "Sexual Identity Development and Synthesis among LGB-Identified and LGB Dis-Identified Persons." *Journal of Psychology and Theology* 33, no. 1 (2005) 3–16.

Yip, Andrew K. T. "Queering Religious Texts: An Exploration of British Non-heterosexual Christians' and Muslims' Strategy of Constructing Sexuality-affirming Hermeneutics." *Sociology* 39, no. 1 (February 2005) 47–65.

Yu, Suee Yan. "The Alien in Deuteronomy." *The Bible Translator* 60, no. 2 (April 2009) 112–17.

CHRISTOPHERYUAN
UNDESERVING OF HIS GRACE • WWW.CHRISTOPHERYUAN.COM

For more information on
the speaking and writing ministry of
Dr. Christopher Yuan:

Website
christopheryuan.com

Email
info@christopheryuan.com

Facebook
facebook.com/christopheryuan

Twitter
@christopheryuan